Come Go with Me

COME GO WITH ME

Old-timer Stories from

the Southern Mountains

COLLECTED BY ROY EDWIN THOMAS

PICTURES BY LASZLO KUBINYI

Farrar · Straus · Giroux

New York

To Robert Calhoun Thomas,
my father, of the Bee Branch community,
Van Buren County, Arkansas
1876–1964
R.E.T.

Text copyright © 1994 by Roy Edwin Thomas
Pictures copyright © 1994 by Laszlo Kubinyi
All rights reserved
Published simultaneously in Canada by HarperCollinsCanadaLtd
Printed in the United States of America
First edition, 1994

Library of Congress Cataloging-in-Publication Data
Thomas, Roy Edwin.
Come go with me : old-timer stories from the Southern mountains / collected by Roy
Edwin Thomas ; pictures by Laszlo Kubinyi.—1st ed.
p.   cm.
1. Ozark Mountains Region—Social life and customs.   2. Appalachian Region,
Southern—Social life and customs.   3. Ouachita Mountains (Ark. and Okla.)—Social life
and customs.   4. Mountain life—Ozark Mountains Region.   5. Mountain
life—Appalachian Region, Southern.   6. Mountain life—Ouachita Mountains (Ark. and
Okla.).   I. Title.
F417.09T46   1994   976.71—dc20   93-45375   CIP   AC

Contents

2

"Momma'd do the best she could"

5

"O-o-oh, that souse!"

6

"When Daddy wasn't a-farming"

7

"We had good neighbors"

11

"They was going somewhere"

Introduction

The stories in this book are told by old, old people who lived in the Southern mountains. They were of the Ozarks and Ouachitas (WA-she-taws) in northwest Arkansas, eastern Oklahoma, and the southern half of Missouri; and of Appalachia south of Pennsylvania in these states: West Virginia, Virginia, Kentucky, Tennessee, North Carolina, Alabama, and Georgia.

I collected these stories in recorded interviews conducted mostly in the 1970s. All but a few of the interviewees are deceased; of those still living, three are over one hundred years old.

The old-timers I interviewed had many stories to tell about growing up in their isolated mountain communities. A hundred years ago, in the days before telephones and radio, long before automobiles and paved roads, life in this region had changed little since before the Civil War.

Families in the Southern mountains depended on one another. They could not rely on the government or private outside agencies for assistance. Folks helped each other when help was needed, and they respected each other's rights. Everyone in the community was expected to do his or her part to make it a safe, pleasant place to live.

Nearly all the people were religious. There were church houses, generally located within a few miles of most families' homes. The early churches were built of logs, and many of them could accommodate no more than forty or fifty worshippers at one time. Baptists and Methodists were the most prevalent, but in many communities, the services were interdenominational because there were not enough members to support more than one church.

Most families lived on farms. Starting when they were not yet six years old, boys helped feed the livestock, and by the time they were ten, many were plowing in the fields behind a mule or horse. Girls learned to cook and to sew and helped in the family garden, where their mother was in charge, and where a large part of the family's food was produced.

Storytelling was more than just a popular way to help pass the time. It also taught children about their heritage. Boys and girls learned to be proud of what their parents and ancestors had done—and to look forward to what the next generation, in turn, might do. Hunting and fishing stories survived for decades. Civil War tales involving family members were still being retold in the 1970s, more than one hundred years after that war ended, and can be heard to this day.

Few people of the Southern mountains had an opportunity to get a good education, but many in each generation advanced economically and socially in a wide array of professional and business fields. They had good reason to be proud of their accomplishments. Their progress resulted largely or entirely from their own efforts.

That has been the American way.

My own family is representative of many families that lived in the Southern mountains.

I was born January 21, 1917, and grew up on a farm at Bee Branch, Van Buren County, Arkansas, in the Ozarks, a community with a population of approximately 150. I had five sisters. My father was the second son and third child of a family of thirteen children. He was a farmer who also taught in little one-room schools, made brooms, and traveled the area selling books to earn money to pay for his children's education. On his horse, in large saddle pockets that were popular at the time, he carried two or three editions of the Bible and a few of the classics to sell. My father's father, a teenage soldier in the Confederate Army during the Civil War, had been a country doctor and Methodist preacher.

My mother's parents were teenage orphans when they were married in 1872. They became farmers and had eight children.

I chose insurance for my own career, after serving in the Pacific during World War II. I was an insurance agent for many years, and in 1961, after earning a doctorate in business administration, I became a college teacher.

In 1970, I started recording interviews with old-timers. I had discovered that there was very little published literature about the old mountain folk culture. My desire to learn more about who I am started me interviewing. My desire to provide a lasting record for others has kept me going. I now have thirteen hundred interviews in my collection.

The selections in this book have been transcribed from the

tape recordings with very minor editing. They are authentic stories from a generation that has passed from the scene. It is my hope that they will be a rich source of information for those with an interest in the folk culture of the Southern mountains, and a source of pride for those readers whose ancestors' lives they reflect.

R.E.T.
Conway, Arkansas, 1993

1

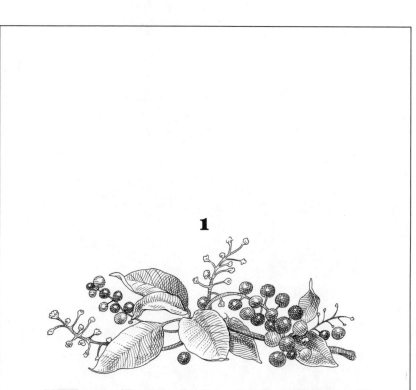

"Where I was born and grew up"

Log Floors in Early Houses

MRS. PEARL THOMAS WILLIAMS

Way back, they'd build houses with green logs. Several men would come to a place after a man had got a lot of logs ready, got them all where he wanted to build a new house. They'd call it a house-raising.

When I can first remember, a lot of the old houses around Morganton [Van Buren County, Arkansas] had floors made out of split logs—white oak logs, most of 'um, I think.

They called that a puncheon floor.

Well, you build a floor with green logs, and when they dry out, they'll be big cracks between the logs.

And I remember a family lived in an old house with that puncheon floor, when I was little.

One evenin', two girls were washing the dishes—I think that was the way it happened—in the kitchen. And they had good-big holes between the logs in the floor. And one of the girls dropped a piece of silverware—a fork or somethin'—through one of those holes.

Well, families back then didn't have much silverware. So

her mother told her to crawl under the floor and get it. So she went under the house. And that girl went under the floor, and bumped her head, and fainted.

And that hole came in handy, 'cause they poured water through there—poured water on her, and revived her.

"Our House"

MRS. JOHNIE GARDNER CRAIG

I'll tell you about our house, where I was born and grew up.

Well, my mother had that house built. She had been married before she and Father married.

Her first husband's health was not very good. And they decided that they would go up in the hills, for they had no family. Leave Woodruff County. They decided they'd go up and live in those hills of Izard County [Arkansas]. Maybe her husband's health would be better.

So they went up and bought a little acreage—about a hundred and sixty acres. And there was a small house on the place, with a huge chimney. Well, they gave orders for the little house to be moved back, and converted into a kitchen, and then to build the main house to this big chimney.

So the house was built, with that kitchen in the rear. The house had a long hall between the two big rooms. Big rooms, about twenty feet square, with a hall between. That was a big house for that time and place, and that was the style of the day.

And the house had a porch the full length, on the front.

It was a log house, of course.

Then later, rooms were added, as the family grew.

Well, that's where Mother and her first husband intended to live. But before they could get the house finished, he died down in Woodruff County.

So Mother got her parents, who had two teenagers—she had a teenage brother and sister—and they came up with her when she moved up there. They came so she wouldn't be entirely alone.

And they lived with her until my father and she were married. And her brother stayed on as the others went back.

Well, as we girls grew up to where we had to have more room, they built a room for us on one end of the porch, and another one into the family livin' room. We had those two big rooms—they were big. You wouldn't believe how many things would go into one of them, and still have room to walk around.

We had an old zinc trunk that stood behind the door. Next to the zinc trunk was a large dresser. I don't know where it had come from. It was an old old thing in my childhood. Big heavy dresser, with a moderately small mirror. The dresser itself had heavy drawers—had three big drawers and a small drawer. Then a mirror above.

And we had the woodbox—where we kept the wood for the fireplace. That was between the door and the window.

And on the one side, up there, there was a bed in that

corner. On the other side, there was Momma's machine, set in the corner. A sewin' machine.

Then the door opened onto the porch. It later opened into a bedroom.

And there was a tall—we called it a sec'etary. It was really a desk with a cabinet on top. That's where Poppa kept all his business papers. And we did our writing and our letters there.

And then Momma an' Poppa's bed was next to that. Under the bed, over there on that other side, was a trundle bed, kept under Momma an' Poppa's bed except at night.

And then, in front of that huge fireplace, we had a big table. We'd take it out in the daytime. We'd bring it in at night so we could study. Have a place for the children to gather around that ol' big table, to study. And that sat in front of the fireplace.

Poppa always sat over on the other side, next to the woodbox. And Momma sat over here with the babies. Over on this part of the room.

Witching for Water

HARVEY WALTER HORTON

Well, the early settlers would try to build their houses close to a spring. We had a good spring where we lived, and we had a good well, too. I know some folks couldn't find a good place on their land to build a house close to a spring. And they'd have to carry water, or haul it, ever so far. Maybe they'd be a quarter of a mile from water, or even further.

My daddy, he wouldn't have a well dug without he knowed where the water was. He'd want a water witch. He wouldn't do it hisself.

Ye see, nobody except one person in a family, gener'ly, could do that, and that's all that can.

Now, I can't. But I had a brother: he could take a little twig and hunt; and have a certain place. And he could stop right there, where the water was, when he came up on it.

I can't find a water vein. But he'd take that stick, that thang he used, a withe. Had a fork in it. He'd hold that in front of him a certain way, and walk around. When he got to the right place, it'd go down to the ground. Yeah, he'd find water.

Sometimes he'd use a peach-tree limb, forked limb. That's what he used. But some of 'um used a straight twig. I've seen it.

Daddy was a Mason; he joined the Masons a way back yonder. And one time he wanted a new well. And he brought a man from the lodge one Saturday evenin' who was a water witch. And he just used a straight stick.

But it's got to be from a fruit-bearing tree. It won't do nothing if it's not a fruit-bearing tree: peach tree, apple tree, and hickory-nut tree.

Well, that feller from Pa's lodge brought his stick. And that twig would go up and down, so many times, till it got to where the water was. And it stopped.

Then he sat down there and counted, holdin' that twig out there in front of him. And every time it would go up and down, wy, that was a foot to water.

When it stopped, he said, "The water's right here; you'll have to go down twenty-eight feet."

Well, he said that's where Pa'd find water, and how far down it was. And that's where they found it, just twenty-eight feet down. That's where we put our well, and where we found water, twenty-eight feet down.

Progress: The First Screens on the Houses

MRS. FANNIE WHITTLE WILLIAMS

Well, I married a boy that was borned and grew up on a farm joining us, on the J. C. Williams farm. We went to school together at Catoosa Springs [Catoosa County, Georgia]. He was twenty-three March the first, and I was twenty-three on October the ninth. We went together . . . well, we was engaged about two years, nearly three years.

Then we got married, and lived in his father's rental house. He was in with his father, farming and making sorghum molasses; and in the sawmill business, together. They owned a sawmill.

And when they weren't working on the farm, they'd cut somebody's timber and saw it into lumber.

Well, anyway, we got married.

And Grandfather said we could live in the house there on the place. It joined my homeplace on the west.

And we newly papered the house, so it would be fresh.

That was in 1905. And that house wasn't screened. There wasn't a house in that valley screened.

My father-in-law had a nice brick house. But he didn't have it screened. The flies was just thick all over.

That's the way it was then, when we married.

And one of my husband's cousins, Johnny Williams, he was a young man. I think he was seventeen years old. And he was a carpenter, a natural-born carpenter. He was a-visitin' Grandpa out there. And he came out to see us.

And my husband asked him if he would make a list of everything it took to screen our house. "I'll go to Dalton and get everythang that you'd want," he told Johnny.

And Cousin Johnny said, "Wy, yes."

And so my husband went to Dalton with Johnny's list, drove a team of mules to a wagon. And he got just a load of dressed lumber that his cousin said it would take to screen our house.

The work took several days. And I'd fix Johnny's lunch— he'd eat lunch with us. And he'd spend the night out at Grandpa Williams's.

And we was just so proud, and so thankful, to have our house screened. The first one in the valley.

Well, pretty soon, the father-in-law got his house screened. And my father over on his farm got screens. And the people all around commenced to having their homes screened.

We was the starter of it.

And after a year or two, most of the families in our valley had screened their houses. And the ones that had would sorter look down on the ones that hadn't. If you didn't have screens on your house, you just wasn't what you should be.

Before we got screens, we'd be afraid to leave any of our doors open—didn't know what would come in at night. We couldn't hardly sleep in hot weather in the summer.

9

But after we got our house screened, wy, in hot weather, we hooked the screen doors, and we could leave the main doors open.

Course that was years and years before we had air-conditioning at home.

The Cat Story

JIM MCGEE

Sixty years ago [1910], we lived in an old boxed house. We had a old wood cookstove. Pa was a preacher, and he was a-setting at the table, a-getting his lesson for Sunday.

And we had a bunch of cats. And one of them was a wild-natured cat. And under that cookstove we had a hole for the cats to go in and out of the house.

And I was setting there. Ma was patching or knitting. And Pa was a-reading the Bible.

And I went and got a little piece of pasteboard and a string. But the first thing I done, I stopped that hole up under the cookstove. And I slipped that string on this wild cat's tail and tied it. Right quick. With one knot.

Course, he woke up and that there paper was a-following him. He run up the wall. Back then, we didn't have the house sealed underneath the joists, just a loft on top of the joists. And that cat run plum across under the roof, on the joists, and down on the other side.

And Father just pulled off his glasses and looked at that cat. He had done lost his piece of pasteboard, you understand.

And while that cat was a-running that run, I pulled the—what the hole was stopped up with—off; and the cat came down and ran out of the house through that hole.

My father looked around, and my mother looked around. And it was, I guess, two or three minutes before anything was said.

Course, I was setting over there, ignorant, ye know. I didn't know nothin'.

Ma said to Pa, she says, "What's wrong with that cat?"

Pa said, "Emeline, I don't know what's wrong with that cat."

And they talked about it for maybe five or ten minutes, about what was the matter with that cat.

And it was a month before I ever told them.

"Ma, Whur's My Bed?"

JOE WARD

They's lots of funny things happened to me when I grew up. One of the funniest things was . . . well, our house—still down there—has got an upstairs. And part of it is the o-o-old original logs. Course, it's been weatherboarded. No telling how old it is. I guess my Great-grandfather Harris built it.

And my two younger brothers and me slept upstairs. My older brother was gone somewhere then. And I slept in one room. And just over in another room, them younger boys slept.

Well, during the day one time, Mother had got up there; and she'd moved the boys' bed from this corner over to that corner.

And as we started up the stairs that night to go to bed, wy —I guess it was me—I said, "Th' last one to bed's a monkey's uncle!"

Course, we was just a-running as hard as we could, ye know. My younger brother got ahead a little bit. And, course, I darted into my room. And he darted in there where he and the youngest brother slept. And when he got where he just thought—it was dark up there—where the bed ought to be, he jumped just as high as he could. But they wasn't no bed there. He just hit the floor.

And he yelled out, "Ma! Whur's my bed?"

You know, most every family has got some of its own little jokes. That's been one of ours for more'n sixty years.

Reading to My Parents, Former Slaves

FRANK WHITLEY

I was thinking about, for myself, the lessons that I got as a child, from my close associations with my parents and their associates. People of their age. They came out of slavery. My father was born in 1849.

One of the things that was important to my parents was: have me to read to them. When I learned to read in school —by the time I was eight, I could read pretty good—they'd have me read to the family most every night. Mainly, I'd be reading out of the Bible.

But there was many other things I read to them. And it was important to them to have me read to them of events of that time.

They were so proud of me.

Following that, they would have company that'd come to see us. Gener'ly, they'd stay all night. And my parents would tell them the stories that I had read to them.

It was an important thing for them; and it was certainly important for me. And not only then, but it give me that emphasis to go on, do some more reading, learn more.

P-S-Y-G-K Spells Pie

MRS. PEARL THOMAS WILLIAMS

I was the eleventh child in a family of eight girls and five boys. Two brothers were younger than me.

Well, Pa was kept busy making a living. He was a country doctor and a Methodist preacher. And Ma stayed busy looking after the home and her children.

So it became customary for the older children to teach the younger ones—it became their responsibility. When I was four years old, they were already teaching me to spell. And one time we were at the dining table, eating. And I asked for some pie.

One of my sisters said, "Pearl, spell 'pie,' and we'll give you some."

That was a new word, and I didn't know how to spell it. But they insisted that I try. And finally I said, "P-S-Y-G-K spells pie."

They gave me some pie for the effort.

And that's the way our Thomas family spelled pie a lot of times for more than seventy-five years: P-S-Y-G-K.

A Girl Starts to School in 1886

MRS. NANCY ANNIE CLINE LUSK

I never got to start to school until I was seven years old.

I had to go through a big woodlands, right out to a creek about halfway. I crossed Indian Creek in an old canoe made out of a log.

My grandfather set me across the creek a lot. They lived not far.

And then I had to walk a quarter of a mile. See, I walked a quarter of a mile to the creek, then another quarter to school. My first school, that was in 1886.

They turned out school at four o'clock. And me and my daddy's half sister went to play at the sandbar by the creek. We tried to build Indian tepees.

The Indians, that's what got that creek that name. Indian Creek. It run into Rockcastle Creek. My father or grandfather set me across the creek; and we played in the sand.

But in crossing the creek to go home one evening, I lost my book. Somebody had give me a primer.

We'd been up with another little girl that went to that same school. It was a big clear place, and we could play and not get dirty.

I laid my book up on a fence corner. And later I couldn't think where I left it.

Well, my daddy had to git a horse, and ride a-horseback

all the way to Beckley [West Virginia], where there was some people that run a store. They run a big store where you had to go for anything. And he got me a spelling book, and a slate and a slate pencil. That's about when I started to school.

When he come back home and give me the book, he said, "Well, that book had better come home."

Seems to me like I can close my eyes and see my daddy say it. He said, "Now, girl, this book had better come home every night."

Baskin's store. That's the name of it. Yeah, up at Beckley. They'd have to go after students' supplies. Took a day to ride there. He had to quit his work and go after me a book.

And I was very careful about that book. He just looked at me, and give orders. He told me what he'd do for me if I lost it. I was sure never to lose that book.

2

"Momma'd do the best she could"

That Panther and the Baby

MRS. EUNICE FOUST SHEARER

I can tell you a story about a panther that I know is facts. You may not believe it.

It was before my day, but it was my aunt. And they was nobody lived in the community, much. The houses was—oh, I guess, eight or ten miles apart. And they was wa-a-ay out yonder close to Drasco [Cleburne County, Arkansas]. I know it was a way back before the Civil War.

They had a little one-room house, log house, with a little window in the back end of it, with a door shutter. And my aunt was a baby. Aunt Tina.

One day, her father had to go to Jamestown to mill. That's over close to Batesville.

Well, he had to go there with some corn to get it ground. And about twelve, he left out, after a shower of rain, to go to mill. He wasn't a-comin' back that night.

So, that evening, after Granny, my aunt's mother, done up her work, milked her cows, she went to bed. And she made her bed down right in the doorway. It was hot weather, you see. And she put two chairs in the doorway.

19

And in the night, the moon was a-shining bright. And they had a great big old house cat. And that cat and a panther waked her up. The panther was a-trying to get through, to get that baby. It was on the other side of her. And Granny jumped up, and knocked the panther out of the house with the chairs, and slammed that door to.

It run around the house. And she knocked it out over there, and slammed that door to. And it run around to that little old window, and she jerked it shut, too.

She said she throwed the baby on the bed. And then the panther commenced trying to come up through the floor. You know, they was great big cracks in the floor. It was a-gnawin' and a-scratchin' right at the cookstove.

It tried to come down the chimney. And she threw a little wood in there, and some stuff, and made a little smoke, and it wouldn't hit that.

And she finally—she burnt it, whur it was a-clawing up, right under the cookstove, a-trying to claw a hole big enough to get in the house. And she just had her a kettle of water, and she got it real hot, and poured it down through there, and stopped that, burnt it.

Then, she said, it got up on the house. And it just clawed and raked and raked.

And daylight come. And Granny said that thing went off down the spring branch—I've been to that old spring hundreds of times—hollering just as loud as it could . . .

It was determined to get that baby, my Aunt Tina.

But now, that's the truth, because I've heard her tell it—Granny—a many a time, how she fought that panther that night. See, it was a new-settled county, and wadn't no houses nowhere, hardly. And the houses that they was, just little old log cabins.

Our grandkids nowadays, they just won't believe that, hardly.

Mother's Two Annual Trips to Town, to Shop

MRS. JOHNIE GARDNER CRAIG

My mother used to make regular shopping trips—now, we lived only five miles from Melbourne [Arkansas], which was our little shopping center—but she made two special shopping trips a year.

In the spring, she went down and laid in material for the children's spring clothes. Well, the spring and summer clothes were all one.

And in the fall, she'd go down and lay in the material for the fall clothes, for fall and winter.

She a-a-always bought two pieces of material for each girl. One was gingham, and one was something else—one was of some thinner stuff. Sometimes she'd get calico, though, instead of gingham.

She always bought a second piece for each girl so she could make a Sunday dress out of it. Lawn or swiss, or something daintier.

And I can remember yet the excitement we girls would have when Momma'd come home, and lay all the bundles on th' bed. An' we'd go through it. An' she'd say, "This is mine, an' this is yours, an' this is yours."

Mother'd pick 'um out. An' she'd tell us, now, if we wanted to swap, she'd let us.

And I wonder now how a woman today would feel with four daughters, how she'd have to go to town and get eight pieces of material, and then have to face all that bunch.

Of course, Momma'd just do the best she could. We never thought anything else. Yes, we never gave it a thought.

Raising Flax for Linen

MRS. ROSA BEASLEY KIRK

When I was a girl, growing up, our family raised flax, to make linen cloth.

And when our flax got ready, we'd cut it. And we'd dry it, and brake it—you'd have to brake it. Take a big pole and lay it across a log and brake it.

You see, the linen strands come in a long, heavy husk of a thing. You hafta bust that hull, to get the fibers out. They say, "Brake it!"

And I've spun a many and a many a thread. We'd use a special spinning wheel to spin linen thread, one a lot smaller than one they'd generally use to spin wool on.

And it makes the purtiest table linens, the flax does. And you just cain't wear one out, hardly a'tall.

And sacks—we didn't have no grain sacks then, like the tow [or gunny] grain sacks that come on now'days. We had to make our own sacks out of flax thread. And they're just as white as a drift of snow.

My mother never did use the loom to make cloth now; but my Grandmother Beasley—Annie Beasley—did. My grandmother and me made grain sacks.

We'd plant our flax, and work it, and take care of it. We'd plant it in rows, just like you'd plant corn, and cultivate it.

And then, when it got ready, we'd get it down—harvest it an' brake it.

We'd beat it, and we'd get it out of that husk—the fine part—and separate the fibers. And then we would spin it into thread. Yeah, we'd spin it into thread.

And we'd weave that thread into cloth. Make sheets out of linen. It's rough a long time. And then the rough will wear off, kind of.

We had sacks. And we had our towels and our underwear out of linen. And Pa would have his drawers made out of it —we called 'um drawers. We'd make Pa's drawers, undershirts, and everything out of flax.

Pa's drawers just came up to the waist, and had a band on them, and a button here—a button in front. And they went down to the ankles.

And we'd put a binding on 'um—we'd put a binding about two inches wide—and make a buttonhole. And when he put his foot in there, he would button it around his ankle. Yeah.

I ain't forgot a bit of it. You don't run up on somebody with a mind as good, to be as old as I am. I'm eighty-nine.

I don't recollect that many folks dyed that linen. Ma never did dye none, only for lining Pa's britches.

You know, Granny was a tailor. And she made all of my father's pants, and coats, and things like that.

And we'd dye with barks, now. Get the bark from different kinds of trees, and dye the linen for the lining of the britches and the coats. Yes, and berries; pokeberries was good, and elderberries. An' then get dogwood and sourwood and white oak bark. White oak bark makes the prettiest pink you ever saw.

And to make dye out of dogwood and sourwood, wy, we'd just whittle off the outside, the rough part of the bark. We'd hew the tree down. And we'd just get the inner bark—just the green bark on the inside. We wouldn't get the old outside part of the bark.

Whiskey Is Good Medicine

MRS. VINA GILBERT METCALF

I've just got one child a-living, and one dead. Me and my husband never lived together but about three years.

He wanted me to sell whiskey, and him make it. And I wouldn't do it. And so he sent me home, to my parents.

And I've been a widow woman about eighty years. I'z seventeen-year-old then.

I believe whiskey is a good medicine, if used with the right thing. But I wouldn't just sell it for people to drink, for 'um to get drunk. No.

One of our Primitive Baptist preachers got about to die with cramp-colic at an association meeting one time. And he was about to die—thought he was going to die.

And they was an old lady there that said—told 'um—that if he'd go up to her house, she'd give him something, if he'd take it, that would cure him.

And he said he'd take anything besides strychnine. That was Preacher Dilley.

And she took him out there, just a few steps out to her house from the church house. And she took him and made him some hot toddy [a drink made from whiskey, water, spices, and sugar] and give him.

And he was ready to go back to the church house in about two hours.

Now, folks could get two kinds of whiskey. They could get what they called dram whiskey. Course, it was bonded whiskey, government whiskey. And they could get the other kind [moonshine] here in Harlan County [Kentucky]. I've heard it said they did.

My daddy got whiskey when he was making his medicine for his family. When he'd get a batch of medicine made out of herbs, he'd get, maybe, a quart or a half a gallon or a gallon. He'd generally make that much at one time. And he'd keep it, just for medicine purposes.

Children and the Asafetida

MRS. CALLIE RAYON WALKER AND

MRS. MARY ARMINTA WILKINSON TRASK

Back when we were little, they didn't have many good medicines, like they do now. And there wasn't hardly any doctors in the Indian Territory, where we lived [in Ottawa County, Oklahoma].

And we used to have to wear them little old asafetidas. Have a string around the necks of the little folks, and a little sack of something or other hanging down. It was a kind of a charm. Oh, it smelled bad!

That was to keep diseases off of us children. I remember having that to put around my neck to keep diseases off. I don't think it did any good. But my daddy and grandmother did.

When I got up about ten or eleven, I just quit wearing it.

Note: These old women had been friends for years, and they shared a room in a nursing home. My notes do not indicate which one made these statements. Each often helped the other with responses—they were almost of one mind.

Early Beds

MRS. EFFIE TURNEY BARNUM DEFOOR

Used to, Ma and Pa had a bed they put up on posts, and put a trundle bed under there, for the kids—the smaller ones —to sleep in every night.

And then we'd have other beds, for the older children to sleep in, when they got big enough to sleep in another room.

Well, that trundle bed wasn't high off of the floor—it was low enough that we'd keep it under the big bed in the daytime. It was fixed on top of four little wheels at the corners.

I think Grandpa Hoggard made our trundle bed. This one. And they'd just push it under the big bedstead.

I guess Grandpa Hoggard made some more stuff for us— I wouldn't doubt it. For I know he cut a pine log and hewed it out, for Pa's horse trough, to water his mules in at night when they'd come in from work in the fields. He could scoop out things like that, out of timber.

And he might have made that big bed Pa and Ma slept in. I just know that we had it, and they said he made it. I never did pay too much attention to it.

But they never did have slats in that big bed, I don't think. I think they tied it together with ropes. And the corners. They made holes on the sides of that big bed and sort of laced that rope across under there. I think that's what they done. See, the mattress rested on them ropes, there.

Ma had lots of feather beds. She made 'um. And she made straw beds. We didn't have no bought mattresses. And she'd empty them straw beds once a year, and boil them ticks [the fabric cases] out. And make us kids fill 'um with new straw. That was a pretty good job, too.

We'd raise the wheat and save the wheat straw. We'd make our straw mattresses out of wheat straw. But if they didn't have any wheat straw, they'd use hay they'd bought for the cattle. They'd just use whatever they had.

Later on, Pa raised oats. And they'd have the oats threshed. And we'd have oat straw for our straw beds.

That was a summertime job. Mother would have the straw ticks emptied, and fresh straw put in. Fresh, clean beds.

An Alcoholic Father

MRS. LULA HARRIS GUTHREY

My father was a fine man. He had lots of friends. But he was a drunkard, and wouldn't stay at one job long. He'd go off to work, and then spend every bit of money he made for whiskey. Wouldn't bring back a thing.

And Grandpa would have to go after us. Bring us in, while Father was gone.

One time he went off and stayed about a year. And Grandpa brought us into his house, or we'd have starved to death. Grandpa had to take us in.

Dad would pretend to git a job. Move us off somewhere and pretend to git a job. And then he'd go off and git another job. He wouldn't like that, and he'd go off and git still another job, and work a little while.

Dad worked on the railroad some. As quick as he'd git a little money, he'd spend it for whiskey. He never would bring nothing back.

And so Mother put up with that as long as she could stand it. And then she quit him.

Mother was sixteen and Father was twenty-one, I think, when they married. But Dad didn't make us a living, and she couldn't stay with him and starve her young ones to death.

My step-daddy was old Uncle Bill Tucker. He was quite a bit older than her. He was—aw!—he was fifty-something, and she was, maybe, thirty-five or forty, or something like that . . . or maybe a little worse. I don't remember.

We saw our father a time or two after Mother quit him, is all we ever saw him. We was living in Marion County [Alabama]. He come down by there. He told some of them he was coming after his children. But he weren't after his children. He just come by, just drunk, a-roving. He weren't a-wanting us. He wanted his whiskey more than anything else.

He was sick. Mother couldn't git him to quit that drinking. She'd beg him to quit.

And he'd promise, "I never will drink another drop, if you'll just forgive me. I'll never drink another drop."

And then go on. Quick as he'd git it, he'd git drunk. Right then. Spend everything he made for liquor. Everything. He didn't give us nothing.

Knitting Stockings and Socks

MRS. CATHERINE FITCH STOUT

The women made the stockings for the family when I was growing up. And sometimes they'd make a double heel—gener'ly would.

And you turned the heel on all stockings and socks. And toed them off just like the men's. But the men's was heavier than the women's. And the stockings for the men and for the women would come right up to the knee.

And to make them so they'd stay up to your knee, you ribbed 'um. I don't know whether that would be what you call it now. You'd knit one stitch this way, and then you'd turn it, and knit under it. And it made a rib. And they'd fit to your leg. They's no give to 'um, much. After you got 'um on, wy, they stayed up.

Some of the stockings for the women and girls would come right up to their knees, and some of them come above their knees.

Well, as the girls would grow up, wy, the stockings would still be good. And you could foot them stockings—knit new feet on them. When the feet would wear out in them, you'd rip those old feet off, and start and knit new feet in them.

And you see, they just lasted. They wasn't like these now. They wasn't a hole ever' time ye put them on. Tear a hole in one, or a runner comes in them now.

Course, they wore long dresses in those days. The girls wore long dresses, down below your ankles.

If I'd have worn a short dress back then? Wy! I'd be the laughingstock, right on and on, for always.

Yeah, I always wore my dresses down about halfway from my ankles to the floor. But I despise 'um too long, to drag the floor.

A lot of them wore their dresses dragging the floor, back them days. Oh, yes! I've seen people—women—they'd have to hold 'um up. They'd have to ketch hold of it and hold 'um up, to keep 'um from dragging the ground.

Making Candles

MRS. ROSA BEASLEY KIRK

Well, we raised a lot of sheep, for their wool. We didn't have no cotton. We just used yarn for our clothes.

We'd shear the sheep, and wash the wool, then pick the burrs out. Well, we took our wool to old man Bonham, and he'd card it in his carding machine.

We had our own spinning wheels—we could spin the thread. And I've wove on the loom. I'm a good hand to weave. Yes, I can weave. We wove all the clothes we wore.

We'd knit our stockings. And we made our own dye, different colors.

I was sixteen years old, the last time I wove any. In 1902. No, I'll take that back. I wove at Pennington Gap, Virginia.

They started a project up there, and wanted people to learn to weave. Miz Nannie DeBusk had a loom, and I was the only one there that knowed how to weave. I showed some of 'um how to weave.

Well, we didn't have any lamps at our house when I was young. We didn't have kerosene lamps for the longest. No. After dark, our light would be from the fireplace, or a pine torch. Or candles.

We made candles. And we had candle lights. No, we didn't have no electric.

First you'd kill a sheep. You wouldn't want the fat to eat, so you'd cut it off—cut off and trim all that fat and cook it in a pot—cook it until all that fat is cooked out. And then strain that fat in a big pan, or something, a kettle. And then let it get cold. You get a big cake that way.

That's tallow. It's a lot different from the fat you get out of a hog—that's lard. Hog lard.

Well, that tallow's not good for many things, except candles. And we'd have some candle molds ready.

You'd put a cotton string, or a wool one, for a wick, in that mold where you wanted it, right in the middle. Then you'd melt that tallow, and pour each mold full of that tallow.

And when it got cold, we'd take 'um out and we had our candles made.

I've made thousands of 'um.

A Girl Stays Home

MRS. LOU BOYD

My mother died when I was young. By that time, my brothers and my sister was married and moved away. Well, they'd all gone, here and yonder, someplace else. I lived with my dad in Arkansas, but my brothers and sister lived in Georgia and Mississippi. I had to stay at home—somebody had to stay with Daddy. And they said I had it to do. I stayed with him a good while.

I wasn't allowed the privilege that many girls was. I was just a self-made girl because I had to learn everything by myself. They'uz all gone but me and my daddy. And a man cain't raise a daughter like a mother can. I take my hat off to my mother.

They's things you can ask your mother that ye cain't ask ye daddy. He was good to me, and all like that. We got along fine; but then, it ain't like havin' a mother. I never was allowed out with young people a'tall. Daddy wouldn't never let me go out with 'um.

But I've lived over it. I had my ninety-fifth birthday last June [1972].

I stayed with my daddy—he died when I was thirty-five. And I got to be a good cook.

33

Woodchopper

MRS. NANCY ANNIE CLINE LUSK

I was born in Tazewell County, old Virginia. And my father brought us to this state. I was between the age of four and five years, in 1883. We moved up in West Virginia, around in Pineville—close by. We settled four miles from Pineville when we come to West Virginia. Wyoming County. I'll live to be ninety-eight years old come the twenty-seventh of May, 1977.

They was eight of us children, and I am the oldest.

I've done all the work they was on a farm, nearly: cooking, washing dishes, washing clothes, milking, plowing.

I've chopped firewood with an old poleax [a single-blade ax] to keep a fire for my mother and the children.

Well, I wanted to chop; and Mother never would allow me to, when I was small. Afraid I'd cut myself.

And they was a lady a-visiting us when I was about fourteen. And she said, "Let her learn to use an ax. She'll be just as awkward when she gets large as she is now. Let her learn. She'll not hurt herself bad."

My father showed me how to chop. And I learned to use an ax like a man.

I never did cut myself with an ax, I don't think, enough to bring blood. I was lucky . . .

Well, I married a sawmill man. And we moved in a house.

And they was a real big hemlock. It was hollowed out at the bottom. I was afraid of that tree.

And I kept trying to get my husband to send a man to chop it down. One day I said to myself, "When he comes in, I'll say to him, if you don't send somebody to fall that tree, I'm going to cut it." And that's what I told him.

He laughed. He said, "I bet you will."

Well, I fooled him. He didn't send.

And when he got back that night, he said, "Who did you get to cut that tree down?"

I said, "I cut it down. I told you I would."

I knowed how to fall that tree, so it wouldn't fall toward the house. And he couldn't hardly believe it. But some of them told him that I really did cut it.

He didn't know I could use a ax.

I didn't tell him nothin' about that before we was married. I was afraid he wouldn't have me.

Making Lye Soap

MISS MARSE AYERS

Well, I've rendered soap—my sister, Lil here, has, too—a lot of times.

In all my years I can remember—I'll be ninety-four years old later this month [October 1970]—wy, we've always had an ash hopper. Well, all winter we'd empty the ashes out of the fireplace and the old wood stove, as long as we had one.

We put the ashes in that hopper. Course, you hafta keep it covered up—you can't let it rain in there a'tall.

And we'd save the cracklings from our lard-rendering [the remains of the fat meat after the lard was removed by boiling] in a jar of some kind if we had it, or something that would hold them.

And when warm weather come, we'd pour water on top of the ashes, let it run through them ashes, and catch it in a little trough at the bottom. Yes, you'd try to wait till that ash hopper was full of ashes to do that.

And you'd pour that lye water—it was just like that old lye you can buy in cans—in a pot. Then put them cracklings in there.

Then you build you a fire under that old black pot, and boil it down. And make soap—lye soap.

I bet I could do it yet.

3

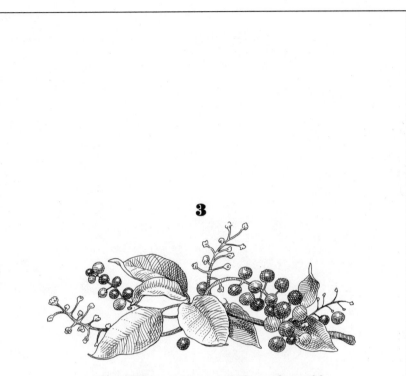

"Daddy was a-plowing"

Ember Days

FRED McCLELLAN

When I was a boy, back eighty years ago [about 1890], they was a bottom over there on Mulberry creek north of Ozark [Franklin County, Arkansas], and we tended the land around it. And on it they was a tree that was a sycamore, a bi-i-ig tree. It had a hole in it about as big as a barrel, down just above the ground.

And while Daddy was a-plowing there, I've went into that tree hundreds of times a day; I'd get to playing around there and go in it. It was hollow, a big hollow tree.

Well, you could take a eight-foot fence rail inside that sycamore tree and stand up, it was that big. You could hold that rail up level about your waist, and turn it around in that tree. It must have been eleven or twelve feet across on the outside, I figure.

And there was a sweet gum tree right close to it. And it was about as big around as that sycamore, but it didn't have no hole. It was solid.

Then an old man bought that land, Old Man Bradbury,

39

Uncle Brad, we called him. The land was just as rich as it could be in the bottom next to the creek. All that land was forest—had trees all over it—and a man couldn't make a living for his family except with the trees cut down and burnt so he could farm it.

The way a feller'd get his land cleared, he deadened the trees in one patch in the spring or summer. And the next winter, he'd go back and cut the trees down and burn 'um up. If you didn't burn 'um ahead of time, they'd be hard to burn next winter.

Well, Uncle Brad knowed just when to go over there—a certain day of month or year—to deaden these trees. He'd go over there and hack around on them with an ax, and deaden 'um. He called it "ember days," when he'd go deaden 'um.

The old man claimed there was two or three ember days in July and August. He'd fix his ax—sharpen it good—and he'd say, "I'm gonna deaden trees tomorrow, up an' down the creek, over in the field."

Well, early the next day, he'd go over there and hit about two licks on that tree with his ax, then go on to the next tree. And that was all of it. He'd cut in two deep hard licks in that tree in the morning, early. And by night, them leaves would be wilted down. Died.

Before next spring, a feller'd try to cut all those deadened trees down and burn them up. If he tried to farm the land the next year after he'd deadened the trees without cutting all the trees and getting rid of 'um, wy, in a high wind, some of 'um's liable to fall. It would be dangerous.

And now, I don't know what days that is, ember days. I guess a feller could get an almanac that would have it in it.

Pretesting a Hired Hand

JOHN PAGE

My wife's grandfather was old Uncle Joe Howard. And he represented Pope County in the early days of the Arkansas legislature. And he owned a lot of land, had a big farm. He hired a lot of people. And he had a method he used of hiring people—he had a system.

They used to say that for the first job, he would put a fellow to turning the grindstone. And they said if when he raised his ax from the stone to look at it, if the fellow kept a-turning, wy, he knew he was all right. And he would hire him.

But if the new fellow would stop turning every time he'd raise his ax off the stone, wy, he knew he was no good. And my grandaddy said he didn't want him around the place.

And that was his system—his standard.

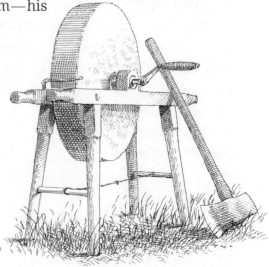

The Unhandiest Things to Carry

GEORGE STACY

You might recollect Uncle Bill Burroughs in the Sand Springs community [Van Buren County, Arkansas]. Folks liked to listen to him . . . you never knew what he'd say.

One time, him and a feller named Harry Bumpers was a-talkin'. So Uncle Bill says, "Mr. Bumpers, now, some neighbors was a-talkin', and they asked the question, what's the unhandiest load you ever carried?"

"Well," Harry Bumpers said, "a load of corn shucks."

Another feller said, "A load of cotton, before it was ginned and baled."

Still another one said, "Na-a-ah, I'll tell ye." He said, "Just loose hay is hard to carry."

Well, then they asked, "Uncle Bill, what's the unhandiest load you ever carried?"

"Well," he says, "I'm going to tell ye. I had a neighbor in good old Alabam'. And he said that the unhandiest load he ever carried was an old poor sow under one arm, and five pigs under the other arm, and enough rails on his shoulder to build a pen to hold 'um."

"Well," Mr. Bumpers said, "that would be considered a bad load, wouldn't it?"

Dad's Yoke of Steers

J. EDWIN TICER

Now, one time, I know my dad had a yoke of steers. They was good big cattle. One of them was an old steer, and the other one was a-getting old. He got them from an old man that raised quite a few cattle. Oh, the old man didn't raise a big bunch, but he had a few around him. And he'd raise steers up to be about three or four years old, ye know, before he'd ever break them to work.

He had some of these big young steers, and he had an old yoke of cattle there. And he had a sawmill, and he logged there, dragged logs with them steers pulling.

He would split these cattle up, separate a team. Then he'd put one of these young steers and the old steer together. But he never did separate them, though, hardly, after he'd worked two together a long time.

And my dad traded for one yoke of them, an old steer and one a-getting old.

In the spring, Uncle John Turner, he just had a right smart-sized crop planted, and he didn't have teams enough to pull the plows. Well, he had a mare and a young mule; but the mare was suckling a colt. And he really needed something else to pull a plow.

Well, I hadn't ever plowed any then. That was in the spring before I was nine years old that fall. That was in 1890.

And my dad told Uncle John Turner, he says, "John, if you'll get a half-yoke, you can take Old Bone, that steer, and put him to a plow. And you plow the mule then, and let Jimmy plow the steer." He had a boy, Jimmy, that was grown, you might say.

Uncle John said, "Wy, you reckon he can ever plow with that steer?"

Dad said, "Yeah, he can plow 'im."

Well, they put that half-yoke on that steer and just put a bridle on him—like a mule or a horse—put it on Old Bone, that old steer. My dad went and helped him with him, a half a day.

And that steer, all the rest of that crop, he'd pull that double-shovel plow around as fast as that mule, and him pulling a single-stock plow. Yeah, he would walk as fast as a mule would.

Old Bone, he was a kind of a long-legged steer—a big steer —and he was one of these kinds of cattle that just wanted to go on. The other steer, he was more of a slow turn; course, you could manage them pretty good when you worked them together, because you generally walked along by the side of them to drive them, anyway.

But that one steer, Old Bone, he just plowed like a mule. It took a pretty-good-stepping horse to keep up.

Note: A double-shovel plow was commonly pulled by one animal. Until about 1890, a plow used in the mountains would make only one furrow. With the double-shovel plow, a farmer could plow two furrows at one time, one blade ten to twelve inches behind and the same distance to one side of the other blade.

The Snake-Chickens

DOC DAVIS

One spring, way back when I was just a little feller, about eight year old, one day, my mother said to me, she says, "Son, go out thar an' see if they ain't some little baby chickens under that ol' hen." She says, "If I've been a-keepin' count good, today—or tomorrow, one—will make twenty-one days since I set that ol' hen. Go out thar an' see if they ain't some baby chickens hatched."

I knowed just where she meant. I'd seen her put sixteen eggs in that nest that she fixed in a old basket that Poppa nailed on the side of the barn, up about three foot above the ground.

Well, I reached down to where that old hen ought to be. And she wasn't in there. And I moved my hand around, a-hoping I'd touch some of them little old fuzzy baby chickens. And I didn't feel no baby chickens, neither.

Down in that nest, where that hen ought to be, they was something that felt very peculiar. Right off, I run over to the woodpile and got a big stick of wood that I could carry, and I set it up right there by that nest. I balanced myself by holding on to the logs of the barn; and then I stepped up on that stick of firewood so's I could look over in that basket.

Bo-o-o-oy! Coiled around in that nest was the biggest old chicken snake I ever saw in my life. He'd swallowed every

45

 one of them sixteen eggs Momma'd put under that setting hen. And it looked like he was just a-staring right at me with his mean-looking, beady old eyes. Lo-o-o-or-dee!

Then I yelled out as loud as I could for Momma to come and help me kill that old snake. It scared her the way I was screaming, and she come a-running. When she come out there, I had an old-fashioned hoe, one with a long handle.

Well, when I disturbed that big rascal, wy, he commenced to try to crawl out of that nest. And when I got back there with that hoe, he had his head a-sticking out, just barely over the top of that old basket, a-fixing to slither somewhere, probably back under the barn.

I got a good grip on that hoe handle and I got the business end of it up about three feet above that old boy's head. It was a long hoe handle. Then I come down right hard with that hoe. It was a lucky hit, and it pretty near cut that varmit's head plum off. It killed him. Dead.

Well, I already knowed a whole lot about snakes, and I sure wasn't afraid of it then. That old chicken snake, it ain't poison, nohow.

Then I brought a ladder out of the barn and leaned it up against the barn wall. And I climbed up on it to where I could see good—course, Momma was terrible scared of all kinds of snakes—and I got a good hold on that old snake's tail. And I lifted it up real high.

And then, right off, one of them eggs chugged out of that

snake. I give that old snake's tail a little jerk, and some more eggs rolled out into that nest. Dreckly, after the eggs quit a-comin' out of that old snake, I could count them. And they was all of them, sixteen eggs. They sure looked a sight, but wasn't none of 'um broke a'tall.

After I throwed that big old snake out there in the tall weeds, Momma come on up close enough to see in that basket. And I said, "Momma, I'm gonna take all a' them eggs in the house an' warsh them in some warm water, clear water, a little. An' then I'm gonna dry 'um good, an' put 'um right back in that nest. I believe they will hatch."

I saw that old setting hen out there a ways, a-cackling.

And Momma says, "A-a-aw! Son, you know they won't hatch after that ol' snake a-swallowing them."

And I says, "I believe they will, Momma. I believe they will hatch."

Well, I warshed them as quick as I could, dried them, and put them back. And as quick as me and Momma got back from that nest, wy, that old hen, sure 'nuff, got back on that nest, on them eggs.

Well, next day, I went back out there and looked in that basket, got back on that ladder and looked in that basket.

And there they was: sixteen of the purtiest little bitty baby chickens you ever saw in your life.

Well, we raised them chickens, and we called them the snake-chickens.

And after that, for the next three or four year, when we'd hear a rooster from that bunch a-crowing, wy, we'd say, "That's one of them snake-chickens a-crowing."

The Hired Hand and the Old Hen

JUD JOLLEY

Old Uncle Jim Riggers lived up on Red Hill, in Van Buren County [Arkansas]. And he only had a one-room log house with a fireplace. Well, they cooked right on the fire. They didn't have no cookstove, so they cooked with a skillet and lid on this fire in the fireplace.

And a old fellow come in here from South Carolina, by the name of King. He settled on some land on the brakes of Hartsuggs Creek. And he and his family was in hard shape. Anywhere he could get a day's work, wy, he'd go work. And he let his kids work the crops at home.

Well, he went up there to work for Uncle Jim Riggers. It was too far for him to go home at night, so he just spent the night there.

One night when he was a-sleeping there, way in the middle of the night, he heard a old hen a-squawling. Well, he never thought but what it was at home. He said the fowl house was just in the right direction to be at home. And he knowed right where he kept his gun a-laying. He knowed he had to go scare off that varmint, whatever it was.

Well, he jumped up and started to reach and get his gun. And he stepped on a bed made down on the floor. And a kid hollered, "Oh, Lordy!"

And he said he just stopped and throwed his head back, and he said, "Oh, Lord, where am I at, anyhow?"

Well, the next day, him and the Riggers boys was plowing. And right on that steep hillside west of Dennard, the patch went right up nearly to that signal tree. And it was awful worrisome to him, for the land was level where he'd come from in South Carolina. And about ten o'clock, they stopped to rest.

He said he thought the boys would like to laugh again, anyhow. And he said, "Well, boys, if that old hen squawls again tonight, she may just squawl!"

The "Mule-colored" Mule

THE HOWARD SISTERS

Our father died in 1893. See, our mother was a widow. She raised six girls. We three, we three old women, are sisters.

Well, we had a fine team of mules on our farm. They were full sisters, just one year apart. Momma raised them.

And so, Mr. Bob Dunlap was one of Clarksville's leading civic-minded citizens. And he dealt with livestock a lot. And he did everything on earth to try to get those mules from Momma. He'd offer her any kind of team. They were considered the finest team of mules in Johnson County [Arkansas].

Well, they were the same size, but different colors. One

was a sorrel, with a black mane and tail. And the other was just "mule-color," ye know. Yes.

The mule-colored one, Kit-Kit was her name. And Moll was the other one. Oh, they were dependable. I'd rather have a mule any day—if I was going to have to work it—than a horse.

And Momma thought the red mule—sorrel—was the prettiest thing. She was pretty.

But Momma sold them.

And about three years later, she ran onto those mules in Clarksville. And before she got to them, they—oh! she was a block away—they began to whinny to her. And they were so jealous, they'd nuzzle over her shoulder, and around. Each one would lay her nose on Momma's shoulder. They were both mare mules.

And Momma, of course, had to weep a little bit.

The Mule on the Bluff

JOHN LEMARR

I don't guess you've heard about that mule a-being out on a bluff after a cyclone, when they found it.

Well, I've heard it. And I guess it could've been so. But I don't know.

It was in Half Moon Valley [Texas County, Missouri]. And it was that same storm that hit St. Louis, about 1892 or '3.

This feller, he lived on the mountain. And he had some land up there.

And down under a bluff in a little valley, wy, his main farm was. And you had to go out the mountain a ways to a gap, to get down, to get to his place under there. And they was a bluff all around that top place.

And he claimed his mule was down in that lower field when the cyclone come.

And the next morning, he was up on top, and nobody hadn't brought him up there.

The mule wasn't hurt.

On Laziness

ROB FARRIS

My grandfather was a farmer. And his farm lay right along by the side of the road. We called it a road, then, just a country road.

Well, he wouldn't stay out of the field, hardly. When it come a shower of rain—he was a real worker—he'd go back, and he'd plow his ground a little wet, sometimes.

Well, there was another farmer lived just beyond him. And there was a little old water mill not far away. Uncle Jesse Goodman had the mill, and run a little store.

And this feller next door liked this water-mill corn bread. And when it came a shower of rain, he'd just, maybe, put a bushel of corn in a sack and put it on his mule. Then he'd come up and bring Uncle Jesse a bushel of corn, to grind. And he'd buy something out of the store.

Then he'd come along in the road right by Granddad's farm.

Well, one day it had stopped raining, and my granddad had went back in the field, to plow. And he'd just plowed out to the fence right here by the side of the road.

And this old man

is riding along on his mule with his corn. My granddad's name was Monford, and people called him Monn. And this fellow said, "Good morning, Uncle Monn." And he said, "Ain't the ground too wet to plow?"

My grandpa said, "It's always too wet or too dry, too hot or too cold, fer a lazy, no-account man to work."

The Automated Barn

AUD SHOFNER

So you want me to tell you about the way my dad had his barn rigged up way back, do ye? Well, see, we're about a half a mile south of the post office here at Damascus [Faulkner County, Arkansas]. And we lived right down from my store here about a quarter of a mile, right down northeast, just below U.S. Highway 65 now.

Yeah. And the house was on the west side of a little branch [or creek], about a hundred feet from that branch. Well, the barn was across the branch—the house was on one side and the barn was on the other. And my dad had a footbridge going to the barn, over that branch, from the house, close to the house. And we'd just walk down there to the barn. There was feed and everything upstairs in the barn. The horses were in stalls underneath.

Course, them days, they'd feed the horses and mules in great big old troughs. Well, Dad just had him a big old box fixed—built there—about two feet square, over the trough.

53

There'd be a box overhead for each horse. He just had two.

He'd put feed in that box overhead of a night; the feed was corn, and hay, too.

Well, the next mornin', he just had a lever, it was in the back room of the house, there. And he'd just go and pull that lever. Ye see, a wire was connected to a peg out in the barn. And he'd go in there and pull that wire, and it'd pull that peg out over in the barn and let that corn and hay fall down fer the horses.

And he didn't have to go down there and feed 'um.

Yeah, rain or shine or nothing. He just had it already fixed. He'd put that feed in that box over the trough—how much-ever he wanted 'um to have. On a cold mornin', that made it nice.

The Goat Fence

JOE LEE WILLIAMS

Uncle Joe Neiman had a bunch of goats one time. I had to keep them out of our wheat field.

And Uncle Joe said to me one time, he says, "Joe, do you want me to tell you how to keep them goats from jumpin' the fence?"

I says, "Law, yeah."

He says, "Just put a plank up and let 'um walk over it."

4

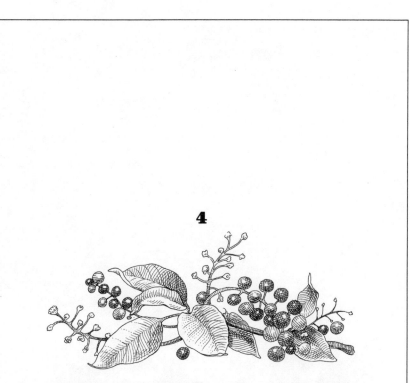

"I hunted all the time I could"

Hunting from a Young Age

LACK CASE

I hunted with my daddy when I was just big enough to follow him. I'd go when I was four or five or six. And I'd carry the game Daddy killed, squirrels mostly.

I'd slip off when I was ten years old, and go stay in the mountains all day, by myself. Maybe I'd kill ten or fifteen squirrels, and get home at dark.

I'd hide my gun out, a .22 rifle.

And I was about eight years old when I started hunting coons.

And after I got grown, after I started my own family, I hunted all the time I could. I've worked six days a week and hunted six nights. And I felt a whole lot better at that time than I do now.

Well now, about health, I'm going to tell ye something. That night air is worth something to anybody that will get out in it. That night air is a whole lot better than the air in the day, if it ain't damp air.

But if ye just go every once in a while, every month or two, it'll kill ye.

But not if ye get used to it, if ye hunt all the time.

The Dog That Climbed the Hollow Tree

JESSE D. HINESLEY

Used to, I hunted anything that they was in the woods. And for a lo-o-ong time, I kept some of the best black-and-tan hound dogs in the country . . . the best anywhere.

And one time, I had me a pretty good dog; and I went over here—I took two dogs—and they treed a fox. And I shot it out.

Well, we went just a little ways from there, and they treed a squirrel, in an old hollow tree. The tree was just like that —hollow top. And a big old hole in the bottom.

One of my dogs got in that hole, and went just like a rabbit, up. And I called him. But he just—every time leaves and trash inside the tree would quit falling—he'd just keep a-going further.

I got me a withe, and split it, and thought I might twist him out. I knowed if he got up there, high in that tree, he'd be into it.

By doggies, he just kept a-climbing, and he went plum up.

Out went the squirrel, before he got up there. It jumped out of the top and run off; and we killed it.

And we come back to that old hollow tree, and that dog was standing out on top, up there. There he was, thirty or forty foot up there.

And it was a big old tree. Yeah, it was two foot through. And it had a crack in it. Leaning.

I had a feller with me. And he said, "Now what are we going to do?"

"Aw!" I said. "I don't know. If I can't get him down safe, I'm going to shoot him down from up there. I ain't a-going to let 'im fall and break his neck."

And that feller was my brother-in-law. And they had to go back to the house and get on the mail car, and go on to Shirley [in Van Buren County, Arkansas]. And I told him, I said, "When you git back to the house, wy, you have that boy of mine and my wife to brang the chopping ax and some of that big wire."

And they come on over. And I got that wire over there—I got that. Then I cut down a sapling and cut the limbs off, and stood it up against that old tree. And I wired this old big dead tree back to another tree. I thought it would brace it some. And you could hear it crack once in a while. I was a-climbing up it, and it was a-popping.

I just kept climbing up that big hollow tree. And finally I got up there, at the top.

And that dog had his hind legs on this side of the tree. And I just grabbed a-hold of 'um both, both hind legs. And he just gave a jump . . . like that.

I hung on to him, and come back down; and handed him to my wife.

Well, he just went to going around and around. And he run back up to smelling that hole. And that boy of mine grabbed him.

I said, "Son, you don't need to get him. He won't go up there anymore."

That's the way it went. He wasn't my best dog, he wasn't too good a dog. I forget now what I called him.

He was just a old black-and-tan hound.

Two Snakes Trying to Swallow Each Other

DAVID L. HAMPTON

I never did see a king snake swallow a poisonous snake; but I've heard people say they did. But I saw two snakes, one time, though . . . They was what I call water moccasins. One commenced at one's tail, and the other one commenced at the other one's tail. And they got their heads as close as they could get them, thataway.

And a fellow by the name of Matt Moody—we was going to school—Matt was with me. We was walking home from school. We heard a noise in the grass. And there was two snakes trying to swallow each other. Their heads, I guess, must have been close as they could get them, not over a foot apart.

And Matt Moody took out his pocketknife and cut their heads off. Moody. They lived neighbors to us.

I guess I was fourteen or fifteen—fourteen, I guess. You might say I was grown.

Now, that don't sound reasonable, two snakes tangled up that way. You may not want to believe it. But if you see Matt Moody, you ask him. He saw it. He'll tell you. That's not been but about eighty-six years. That was back in 1887 or 1888.

Matt Moody saw it. He'll tell you.

Uncle Mary

FOLKTALE, RELATED BY A MR. BEALE

My daddy had a neighbor way back who was an old man, and he loved to go fishing. And every weekend when weather and his farm work would permit, he would hitch up his team of mules to his wagon and go down to a little creek about five or six miles away, for the weekend. He'd try to be ready to leave at noon on a Saturday. And he wouldn't never come back home until late on Sunday night, hardly at all.

Well, he'd stop his wagon right close to that creek, close to a good fishing hole on the creek. And then he'd take his mules loose, take their harness off, and hitch them to the hind wheels, with some hay in the back end of the wagon, or under it, for them to eat on.

Course, he'd put a pallet under the wagon and sleep on it at night, or maybe rest on Sunday after dinner when it got hot and he got tired.

Then he'd get his fishing lines and hooks and bait—he'd dug his bait back at the house before he left—and go down

there and drop his hook down in the water.

Now, Uncle Mary—his name was Marion, but my daddy called him Uncle Mary when he wasn't around—Uncle Mary was a good fisherman, don't you forget it. He'd nearly always take some fish home. I remember one time he caught two big catfish and took home right at twenty-five pounds of fish. He sent a good mess over to our house, I recollect.

Well, some of his neighbors—four or five men and big boys—decided to have a little fun with Uncle Mary. So they made it up to go down there, late one night, after they knowed he'd be sound asleep. They got down there, and he was snoring. They slipped in there, and unhitched his mules and led 'um off a little ways and tied 'um up good.

There was three men in on it—I guess they was just three of 'um. And all of a sudden, they started yelling as loud as they could, "It's a runaway! It's a runaway! It's a runaway!"

And this old feller was about half-awake from his sleeping. And he suddenly thought something bad was about to happen to him. He was still half-asleep; he couldn't understand what was a-taking place.

So Uncle Mary, he jumped up, butted his head a couple of times against the bottom of that wagon, and finally got out from under it. And he lit out a-running away from all that noise them three fellers was a-making—like they figured he would—and he tore out across down through there. And he landed slap in the middle of that big hole of water.

Course, that woke him up good, I'll say that.

And they never did let on to him who it was. And he never did say nothing to any of 'um about it.

Fiddling for Fish Worms

ANONYMOUS

One time, my father was getting ready to go fishing with a man. They didn't have any bait yet.

And Father told that man that you could—that he could —fiddle him up some worms for fish bait.

And this man thought Pa was crazy—he'd just moved into our community.

That was up on Brindlee Mountain [De Kalb County, Alabama].

Well, Pa drove a good long stob [or stake] in the ground whur he thought they'd be some red worms. And he'd take a rough sand rock, or a rough board that hadn't been planed. And he'd saw it backwards and forth across the end of that stob that was stuck in the ground.

He'd drive that stob down in the ground, a foot or so. Then seesaw with that heavy rock, across, ye know, to jar the earth. To make the earth vibrate.

Pretty soon, here would come these big worms out of the

ground, for fish bait. Yes sir, the worms would come up out of the ground. I watched them. I know just how he did it. And he called it fiddling up worms.

Girls Went Fishing with Their Brother

MRS. MECY RELOFORD SINGLETON

I had one brother, and he liked to fish. And us girls always went fishing with him.

Well, the only way we ever fished was with a line—pole and line. And I've fished a many a time with just a bent pin for a hook—I shore have.

And the biggest fish we ever caught—I seen a woman that caught a big red horsefish on a pin, for a hook. It broke the line, the pole, and got back in the water. Oh, it was a foot and a half long. We was a-fishing together that time.

And she said she wasn't fishing for red hosses—she was fishing for minnows, she said. She called it a "red hoss."

It was on the Fourth of July.

Not everybody could dress a red horsefish. They have a sight of bones; and you couldn't hardly eat 'um without they was cut up just right. They had a real good taste.

I didn't fish for just one kind of fish. But I caught a lot of fish. And I used to catch a lot of turtles. They'd get our bait, ye know.

We never would save the turtles. My mother was a funny person that way. She wouldn't eat a turtle, nor a bullfrog,

64

nor nothing like that. She wouldn't eat a eel. I did, though —I ate eels. I thought they was good. Mother said they looked too much like a snake.

We had a neighbor when I was growing up that ate every turtle he could get. He said they was awful good.

And one of my cousins—a McKinnon—he would kill bullfrogs to eat. He was an awful fisherman, and he'd save everything that he'd get thataway. Bullfrogs, turtles, eels.

I've seen bullfrog legs frying. They'd move around in the skillet.

And my father used to talk about one of his sisters. He said when she'd be a-frying frog legs, she said that they would move in the hot grease, and she'd cry. I've heard other people say they'd do that, too.

The Fight: Coon and Dog

CLIFTON CLOWERS

There used to be a big hole of water in a creek not far from here [Woolverton Mountain, Conway County, Arkansas]. And there was a big old coon, he had a home out there in a big tree not far from that big hole of water.

And hunters would take a dog down there, and he'd get after that big coon. And the coon'd run around, get out of the way for a while. And then he'd take off to that big hole of water. Jump in.

And whenever a dog got out there, swimmin' after him,

that coon would just climb up on a dog's head, and he couldn't do nothin' with him. And he'd just hold that dog's head under the water. And they lost two good dogs with him. He drownded them.

And a feller over there, he was an old hunter, he said, "I've got a dog that it won't hold his head under the water."

They said, "When could you come down there, and us go a-hunting, and see what he will do with that thing?"

He told them when he'd be down there. And he come. And they all went over there to the old tree where the coon denned. And he'd done come down, and gone off in the woods.

And that old dog hit his track. He trailed him around and around. And finally the coon got tired of it, and he went back to his hole of water. And he got out there.

And this old dog, when he got to the hole of water, he jist piled in there, and went out there to that coon. And the old coon, he jist piled up on his head.

When he did, that dog jist started going right fast toward the outside, where them men was, with that coon on his head. And the old coon jist stayed on him. They got out of the water, and he went out there, right nearly where the men was at, watching them.

And that old dog jist finally got the old coon off of his head, and he throwed it on its back, and got it around the neck. And he never did turn it loose. He choked it to death.

A Wild Turkey Caught, Barely

WILLIAM COLUMBUS SMITH

I was borned at Bruno in Marion County [Arkansas], not far from the Searcy County line. That was on August the second, 1880. Well, my father died. I was born in August, and my father died in April the next spring.

And my mother moved us back to Newton County. That's whur she was raised. And I growed up in Newton County, up there.

We moved back, up the Little Buffalo River, above Jasper, about five miles. Well now, right there at that cave—Diamond Cave, just below it—was whur I growed up to be about . . . oh, I don't know. I growed up to be a great big boy. I don't know how many years I might have been, and so on. But that's whur I growed up at.

And then my mother married again. And we moved on up the river, above Mount Par-THEE-non. They just call it PAR-the-non, now.

Well now, my stepfather was a great hunter, had been. But he couldn't hear very good after I first knowed him. And that's the way I learned about hunting . . . going with him so's I could listen to the dogs barking, and help him go to them when they'd tree something.

And I remember going with him one spring morning, when I wasn't no more than eight or nine.

Well, the previous evening, we was planting corn. And they was a big old turkey gobbler got to gobbling around. About sundown, we went on home.

Next morning, about three or four o'clock, we was up and on our way down there. And we got there, and commenced to wait fer that old gobbler to gobble, down there.

And we got pretty close to whur we thought he'd be before we ever stopped. We didn't know whur that he roosted at. We just knowed that he was a-going to roost there, somewheres. And we got down in the field at that time, just a little before it started getting light.

And pretty soon, wy, he reared up and gobbled.

Well, I had to go to hear fer the old man. And I told him whur he's at, whur he's gobbling at. Then we went on a piece. We had to be very careful, and not make very much noise. A gobbler scares easy, ye know. And we slipped up on him.

The old man was using a old muzzle-loading rifle, cap and ball, you called 'um.

Well, we got up there, and we set down there and watched him. And we could see him up there, strutting backwards and forwards on the limb of a big sycamore tree. And it got light enough for him to see how to see and my stepfather shot him. But he shot him too low down, too far back: he broke one leg.

That gobbler pitched across the hollow and lit down by the side of a old log, and just squatted. Course, it made him sick.

And we slipped up there, on him. We was way up towards the top of the hill, from a branch.

We got up there, and the old man shot him again. And that

time, his gun made cap fire—long fire, they called it. The cap busted. The report of the cap was before the gun fired. And that old turkey gobbler wiggled off. And it just broke one wing, that second shot. He had one leg broke, and one wing broke.

And of course, that gobbler jumped out and started to running. And I took in after him down at the foot of that hill, down there. And I caught him. I caught him right by the neck.

And boys my age back then, they wore waist-pants: short britches, and we buttoned the pants to the waist.

When I caught him by the neck, wy, I kind of reared up with him. He caught in the top of that waist with that good foot. And he stripped all them buttons plum down there, and stripped my britches off.

And I got a stripe down my breast, whur that toenail raked it.

And the fellers, when I tell them this story—I been a-telling it fer eighty years now—  they nearly always ask me, "Didn't ye turn that gobbler a-loose on account of losing them buttons, of losing your britches?"

And I'll tell you about that. No sir! I didn't turn it loose. No-o-o! I wouldn't have turned it loose at all. I stayed right there on top of him. And whenever that I got on top of him, then—course, my britches was off—wy, then I stayed with him till the old man got down there and got him.

That's—as the feller says—that's a terrible tale for a preacher to tell. But it's thataway.

Leave a Hornets' Nest Alone!

LELAND DUVALL

Back when I was a boy, there wasn't much for us to do, and we got interested in hornets. And we'd go up and down the creeks, looking to find out where they'd hang their nests. They was hard to find, but once in a while, you'd find one.

And my cousin and I, we were always running around, you know—we were ten or twelve years old—and squirrel-hunting, and one thing and another.

And every time you'd find a hornets' nest, it was a challenge. That's what it amounted to. We learned real quick that you couldn't throw rocks at a hornets' nest. I don't care if you got back as far as you could throw, when you threw a rock at a hornets' nest, they would find you, see.

Now, a wasp won't do that, or a yellow jacket. But as far as you can throw a rock, a hornet can come back where the rock came from. He'll find you. He'll get you.

We discovered that, and we quit that real quick after we got stung once, throwing rocks at a hornets' nest.

Then I remember, we found a hornets' nest over on Isbell

Creek [Pope County, Arkansas]. Great big nest, hanging on a sweet gum limb, up there.

And we had two dogs, two squirrel dogs. One of 'um would tree, and the other wouldn't. He wasn't any good. We was mad at him because he wouldn't tree. We was also mad at him because every time we shot a squirrel, he would grab it up and run off with it if we didn't hold him. That was one of his bad habits.

We thought, Boy, we'll fix him. So we backed up and lay down behind a drift in the creek bottom, well hidden from that hornets' nest.

And we got to shooting at this limb with a .22 caliber rifle. The nest was hanging on a limb. And dreckly, we shot it down.

And this old sorry dog, the one that wouldn't tree, we were mad at that dog. So then we turned him loose.

Well, this dog, he thought we'd shot another squirrel out of the tree. And ma-a-an! Did he go after it!

But when he got down there to that nest, of course, those hornets just covered him up. And what we hadn't counted on—as soon as they started to stinging him, wy, he turned right around—and he come right straight back to us. And he brought the whole bunch of hornets with him.

Now, that probably never happened to anybody else in the world. But it sure did to me and my cousin.

5

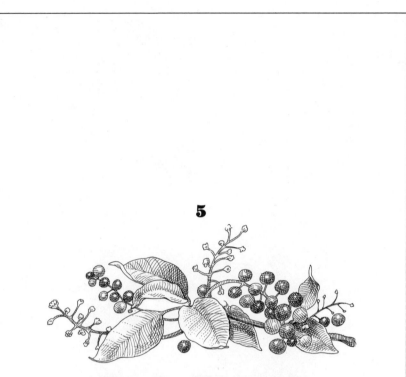

"O-o-oh, that souse!"

Souse, Also Called Headcheese

MRS. EMMA SMITH HESS

O-o-oh, that souse! You could jist make a meal of it. But it don't keep long.

Now, I'm gonna tell ye how to make it.

You took the head of a hog, and feet and ears—and cleaned 'um. And after ye got 'um ready, you cooked 'um till they was perfectly soft. Then you'd pick out all the meat from the bones. Then you either mashed 'um or run 'um through some kind of thing, a colander, something with holes in the bottom. You put a press on it and all the water and grease would drain out.

An' that was souse. It was just like cheese. You could cut off a big slice, put sage on it . . .

We've killed lots of hogs that weighed four hundred pounds. In the early days, some of 'um wasn't too fat, like they are nowadays. I reckon ye could make maybe a gallon of souse out of a 400-pound hog.

Food in the Smokehouse

OSCAR UNDERWOOD

Way back, every family would have a smokehouse. Course, it would be made out of logs, with a wood-shingle roof. That's the way nearly all the buildings was built, back then.

Well, the way that it got its name, we'd have to have a place to hang our meat to smoke it. Hog meat. Pork. I don't think we ever dried and smoked any beef in there, I don't think we ever did. We'd only kill a beef every once in a while. But we didn't think we had much to eat if we didn't have some kind of pork on the table, the dining table, at mealtime.

We used hickory wood, and sassafras, to smoke the meat. Mother liked hickory best for smoking meat; but Daddy said he liked a variety, and sometimes he'd smoke it with sassafras. We'd have an old zinc tub down there, or a kettle of some kind, down on the dirt floor in the smokehouse to put this wood in—whichever it was.

And the meat would be a-hanging up there above the wood that's a-smoking. And the smoke would go up amongst it, and it would smoke it brown, and put it in fine shape. It would have a good flavor after three or four or five days.

The smokehouse is the place where Mother kept her lye soap. She'd have a great big old barrel of soap there, right by the door. And by the other side of the door, that's where we had a big old barrel that we kept our molasses in it. It would hold, I guess, a little more than fifty gallon, and lots of years we'd fill up with 'lasses when we made it early in October.

And my wife's mother had a loom that she kept in their smokehouse. It was warm enough built that she done all the clothmaking in there in the winter. And she wove all their clothes in there. It was cool in there in the summer, because it was a dirt floor.

And that's what some families kept in their smokehouses.

Goat for a Neighbor

MRS. BETTY ROGERS BYRD

Our family kept cattle and hogs and horses. And my daddy kept a bunch of goats. They wasn't milk goats. They was just goats that you could kill and eat.

Lots of times, on the weekend, if we knew we was gonna have company, we'd kill a goat and cook the whole thing. They ain't much of them after you get them skinned, or they wasn't ours. They were little, kind of a small kind.

Well, my father or one of the boys would kill a goat and dress it. Then we'd put it in water and boil it—in salt water. And put a pod of pepper in there with it. Cook it in a big pot on the stove, or in the fireplace.

Then we'd take it out of that salt water, and put it in some fresh water to try to get some of the salt out.

We had a big Willard Range cookstove—got it about 1889 or '90. And we'd put the goat in a pan, a great big pan, nearly three foot square. We'd put it in the pan and bake it after we had boiled it for an hour or two.

Goat meat has got a different taste from anything else. Yes, than anything else. But all our family liked to eat it.

And we used to have a neighbor that—aw! she wouldn't eat goat.

My daddy looked out the window one day and saw her comin' to our house. She often would come and stay all day. We had cooked a goat that evening before.

And Daddy says, "Yonder comes Miz Hayes." He says, "Now, that's not kid, that's sheep." He wanted us to tell her that meat was sheep, and not young goat.

So she just ate the biggest dinner, and took on about the meat. She said it was the best mutton she ever ate in her life.

And after she got through eating, my daddy told her what it was.

"Well," she said, "I'll never say nothing more about folks a-eating goat." She said, "I'll eat it, too, from now on."

Cooking Coon

MRS. BETTY ROGERS BYRD

My brothers hunted. They shot rabbits; back then, they wuzn't no disease among the rabbits, and they wuzn't no law against it. They hunted squirrels, too. And they brought coons and possums home, for me to cook.

See, I was the oldest girl in the family, and I did the cooking for our family after Mother died.

I knew just how to cook all the wild game my brothers caught.

Well, the hunter that brings in the game is s'posed to dress it. That's an old rule.

You put a coon in a big pot of water, and put it over a fire an' boil it, with salt and pepper. Boil it until it's pretty tender. And you boil sweet potatoes.

Then you grease ye a pan, and lay ye coon in there—of course dressed, but not cut up—and split ye sweet potatoes, an' lay 'um over it. And if that coon don't make enough seasonin'—if it's not very fat—then put some bacon strips across your potatoes, and let 'um bake. After they've baked awhile, wy, you've got a big meal.

I never liked possum. It'uz too fat. But th' coon wuz different. Th' coon wuz good. But, course, there was some folks that liked to eat possum, an' wouldn't eat coon a'tall.

Cider Making

MRS. EMMA SMITH HESS

We had a good cider mill, and we had a good fruit orchard. We used to raise a turrible lot of apples. And we made cider and vinegar.

It takes a sour apple to make good cider and good vinegar. My daddy and my grandpap set out lots of apple trees, several different kinds.

Now, the cider mill, I'll have to explain it. It's pretty complicated.

It had a big screw that come up here. Turned around and around. And it had a round thing on the bottom, down here. Just like a setscrew. But it was—oh!—two foot long.

Well, it had buckets. They stood up endways, and was made of staves [of wood] with steel or iron rims around them. Just like a barrel, but both ends was open. And this cider mill had a crank to it. And it had a wheel in there that had teeth in it. It would cut these apples all to pieces. Well now, these buckets set on a platform under this mill. They were fastened to the platform. And you'd pull one bucket up under where you was grinding. And you'd cut and grind them apples until you'd fill that bucket with juice.

The other bucket, you'd catch the pieces of apples, after they'd had the juice separated.

And when you got a bucket full of that juice, you'd pour it in a tub.

Well, you could keep on making that cider—cut the apples up and squeeze the juice all out—as long as you could have somebody turning that crank. Course, you'd have somebody cut the apples into quarters, and feed 'um into that cider mill. And when you needed to empty a bucket, you'd stop turning.

Well, after you've got your cider made—cider is just apple juice—then you're ready to make your vinegar. You have to have it set a certain length of time, and it will sour. It might take months—a month anyway.

I've heard you could make something pretty strong out of that cider—set it out and just leave it. Course, you wouldn't never have any cider to make into vinegar or wine until along in the fall, when apples got ripe, the kinds that made good cider. By then it'd begin to get cool weather, and the cider wouldn't sour so fast.

Poke Sallet and Green Onions

MRS. ALICE HODGE McGUIRE

We were glad to know when poke sallet and green onions were big enough to eat in the spring. Course, I usually had green onions from my garden the year around. I never did have to bother with wild onions. But a lot of families would gather them in the spring, to eat.

I've canned a lot of poke sallet, to have to eat at different times of the year. You can gather it only in the early spring.

Well, the way I did, I parboiled it in salt water. And then I'd wash it. Then I just fried it, seasoned it, in highly seasoned bacon grease.

But I liked to mix that poke sallet with turnip greens, or mustard greens, cook them together. Yes, I thought it improved both of them to mix them. We liked it that way.

Note: The pokeweed grows wild in several Southern states. The root is regarded as poisonous, but in early spring the tender young shoots can be cut and boiled, to be served as table greens.

Molasses Contest

FRED MCCOY

I used to be good at making sorghum molasses. Real good. And they had been some other fellers that made 'lasses that thought they was good, too. One was Andrew Neal. And he had a cousin who made 'lasses. We all made it down there . . . we'd put our mills up by that spring on the old Ben Bennington place.

My father-in-law had started making sorghum there first. The place where I put my mill was directly under a big limb of a giant black gum tree that had growed up close to the spring.

Well, Andrew used to brag a whole lot; and one day he commenced to claim how much better his sorghum was than ours. And so we all hung up little samples of bottles with the molasses in it to a limb of that big tree. And so that would let anybody that come there test and see who could make the brightest, prettiest molasses.

First, John Neal, Andrew's cousin, made some, and he hung up a bottle of good molasses. Andrew had, too, and he hung up his bottle.

Here come my turn. I went out and got me a bottle, then went to the charcoal pile there . . . and crumbled some of that charcoal as fine as I could and put it in my bottle. And the skimmings [dregs removed from the boiling sorghum juice]—we had a hole in the ground that we put the skimmings in. I got some of that and filled up my bottle with it. And I hung it up.

And you couldn't see through it no more than you could see through leather. It just looked like leather.

Well, I didn't think anybody would taste of it. But that pair thought I might beat 'um making molasses. Course, they didn't know what I'd done.

Andrew Neal, he come out to visit about the time we'd made one pan of 'lasses. You'd generally make a couple of pans a day.

I had my sample up there with those others. Andrew looked at them, and he said, "Huh! Whose is this?"

I said, "It's mine."

He said, "It's awful dark, ain't it?"

I said, "It's not only dark, but it's just black." I said, "Boy! It's good."

Then he just took my bottle down and—I didn't want him to, but I couldn't stop him—and he tasted it, them skimmings and coal.

I knowed they wouldn't hurt him, even if he swallowed some.

But I didn't think he was going to take hold of it, and taste it.

A Five-Year-Old Blackberry Picker

ERNEST CLINE HALTEMAN

Never was much money for us boys. There wasn't many ways we could get us some cash to spend.

The first money I ever earned, I'll tell ye about that, I never will forget it. I bet I wasn't over five years old.

Me and my brother picked a gallon of blackberries apiece. And we carried 'um to town, about four miles, to Mrs. Cooper. And she give us a nickel a gallon. She had the boardin'house then.

That was my first money to spend for what I wanted.

Well, I know just exactly how I spent that five cents.

Kenneth Rivers was a-runnin' a store down there. And I went in the store and told him—I forget what kind of tobacco it was—I wanted a piece of tobacco. He was kinfolks to us.

And he was about to get onto me. He wanted to know what I was a-gonna do with it. I says, "I'm a-gittin' it fer my granddaddy." And I was!

He let me have it. And I tuck it to him.

Sugarless Cake

MRS. LIZA ANN CARTER SMITH

I do like corn bread. I had corn bread last night at this nursing home [in Lewisburg, Greenbrier County, West Virginia]. I had corn bread for supper, white meal.

My husband would not eat corn bread when he married. But I put some on the dining table for me.

He looked at it and said, "What kind of cake is that?"

"Oh," I said, "that's the best cake there is." I said, "That's sugarless cake. You don't have to put sugar in it."

He said, "How in the world did you make cake without putting sugar in it?"

I said, "I made it out of meal and flour. You taste it. It hasn't got a bit of sugar in it."

Lord! Then he jumped on it. I never got hardly a bit of it.

After that, we'd both eat it. I'd bake enough corn bread for both of us.

And I kept calling it sugarless cake, for him.

Preserving Sausage

EZRA ADDINGTON

We had some glass jars when I can first remember. But they'd usually have crocks that they'd put their sausage in. Old-time crocks. And Mother would put her sausage in a gallon crock. There was a big family of us. And we had an awful lot of company. Daddy was a pretty successful farmer, and had a lot of cattle. And cattlemen would ride through the country, and they always stopped at our house.

Anyway, Mother would fix that sausage. And then she'd melt her lard—when she rendered her lard—and pour all over the top there a coat of that lard on the sausage, to keep it airtight. Then put a lid on it.

And when she opened that sausage, wy, she'd take her knife and cut it out, take what she wanted. And, course, we'd use it up in a few days.

Another way they'd do, Grandmother Addington, now she was older—she was Father's mother. She would take a new cloth, white cloth, and make these bags, and stuff her sausage down in that. And then tie the top real tight. And dip this in that hot lard. And what lard stayed on that would harden, and she would hang it up, where she wanted to store it. Hang it up out of the way of rats and anything.

When she wanted her sausage, she'd go get that, and cut it. It would be round, when you'd stuff that bag full, it would be in round rolls. It was kind of like they put it up now, what you see in the stores. Cut it off in cakes and cook it.

Later, they got to storing the sausage in hogs' intestines, later years. But our parents . . . I don't remember them ever doing it.

"That's the Way I Like It!"

FOLKTALE, RELATED BY LELAND DUVALL

There were seven boys and two girls in the Garragus family which grew up in the Hector-Scottsville area of Pope County [Arkansas]. The first children must have been born before the Civil War, or during it.

The youngest son was named Jake; he was born in 1874. When he was about ten, the mother of that family died. For a while, the two girls took care of the cooking and other housework. But by the time their father passed away, the girls had married and started their own families. That was when Jake was age nineteen, in 1893.

Well, that left at home—for four or five years, I guess—about four or five bachelor brothers living together.

None of the brothers wanted to cook; but it was necessary for one of them to do it. So they decided to draw straws—straws from a broom, the unlucky one would be the one that drew the shortest straw—to see who would start out doing the cooking. And they agreed that he would have to keep doing the cooking until one of the other brothers complained about his cooking, or volunteered to take it over. Once a brother got the job, he would have to keep it until one of the others complained about his cooking.

Thus, one of them was chosen to cook. And after he had cooked a few days, he decided that somebody ought to complain. Nobody had.

So he started to make corn bread one evening. And he just —instead of putting the normal amount of salt in there—he put a handful in.

And that was George Garragus who was doing the cooking then. Yeah, he put a handful of salt in the corn bread, cooked it, and put it on the supper table.

And so Jake, he took a bite of corn bread. And then he said, "That's the saltiest corn bread I ever tasted . . ."

Suddenly he remembered the rule about the complainer having to take over the cooking chores. And he added, real quick, "And that's exactly the way I like it!"

6

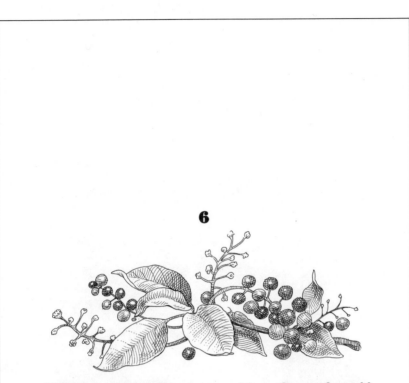

"When Daddy wasn't a-farming"

Woman Helped at Her Husband's Sawmill

MRS. NANCY ANNIE CLINE LUSK

My husband was a sawmill man. Bought him a sawmill when he was eighteen.

I even worked some at that sawmill.

One time, he was a-cutting timber for the Edder Cup Coal Company. And they needed some timber in a hurry at one of their mines.

Well, they come to him and told him that if he'd finish their order that week, they'd give him five dollars more on the thousand board feet.

Well, one day that week a fireman showed up in a bad way. Couldn't do the work, couldn't hold enough steam to keep the saw a-going.

His cousin was a-running the cutoff. And they wouldn't be able to saw till they could find somebody to fire that engine.

Well, I was big and strong. And I'd learned what the fireman has to do. And I said, "I'll go down there. I'll fire that engine."

And some of 'um laughed.

But the cutoff man said, "Come right on. I'll fix the wood so you can handle it."

I said, "Now, I won't fool with the boiler. You'll have to look after that. But I'll keep that fire a-goin'."

I fired that sawmill engine, and helped saw that day. We was just squaring up big timbers.

And my husband had two big old trucks. When they got all that timber sawed and ready, they had nobody to drive one truck. Now, I'd learned to drive anything: an old wagon, or wheelbarrow, or horses, and stuff. And I'd learned to drive a truck, and cars—anything that had wheels on it.

I said, "Well, load it up. Jist load the ton-and-a-half truck up. I'm ready."

Well, they got the two trucks loaded. And we started over to whur the schoolhouse was. You had to go across the railroad to go up to town, whur you unload it. I stopped there, and the other truck was a-following me.

"Well," I says, "I won't go down this way, up through town. You can unload yours, and come back and git this one."

Ye see, we hadn't got nowhur till the men commenced to hollering at my husband, laughing at him for having his wife a-driving one of them trucks.

My husband said, "Ann, I thought you was going to drive one of the trucks over there."

But I wouldn't go through town, driving that old ugly truck.

That happened in Davy, McDowell County, West Virginia.

Well, they got the bonus from that coal company. And the superintendent of that coal company said that I ought to have the five dollars.

Peddler Morris

JIMMY DRIFTWOOD

My Grandfather Morris was a little too young to get in the Civil War. They wouldn't take him. They lived on Buffalo River, Spring Creek of Buffalo River [in Arkansas]. And he showed me the bi-i-ig sycamore tree that he'd go to each morning before daylight, to hide. They was a big hollow root of that sycamore down at the creek, and he'd crawl up in that. He had holes bored in that root, to see out.

The reason he had to go under there and hide each day is that the desperadoes, the bushwhackers—the jayhawkers, we called them here—they would kill any boy that was big enough to kill them. They needed to get rid of him.

And while Grandfather was in this tree, he studied about music. And not long after the war ended, he went to New York to study music, and voice, and he became a singing-school teacher. He became a great singing-school teacher. He even went into Indian Territory, what's now Oklahoma, and taught singing schools. And he had a store out in Rich-woods, a few miles south of Mountain View [Stone County, Arkansas].

And Grandfather tried to operate water mills, to grind corn into meal. But he never did seem to be able to have success business-wise.

Finally, he got so old he couldn't teach singing schools.

95

But he had to have something to do. So he started peddling. He had a wagon and a team of mules, took along goods the country people needed. He'd trade his goods for the country people's chickens and eggs. And he'd just go all over the country.

Back then, each community had a telephone system of its own. And when he arrived at a house, they'd soon pass out word on the old party line. Everybody was invited, and they'd have a big singing wherever he stopped and spent the night.

Grandfather was an excellent musician; he specialized in the organ. That was his favorite instrument. And he had a fine voice. Wherever and whenever he stayed all night, they'd take their receivers all down on the old telephone party line. They could all hear Grandfather playing the organ, and they'd sing along, unless they could go to where he was staying and join the party.

The family he stayed all night with would give him free lodging and feed his horses or mules, for the entertainment.

Note: Bushwhackers were outlaws who refused to fight with either the Union or the Confederate Army but who roamed through the country heavily armed, stealing, burning, torturing, and killing innocent people while all the men and big boys were away in the war.

Making and Selling Chairs

WILLIS WARREN

My daddy was mainly a farmer. He raised corn and cotton and wheat and oats. Sorghum cane, too, and so on. And he was a big bee man. He had about forty hives of honeybees on the old place up till about two years before he died. I bought 'um after he got so's he couldn't look after them.

Well, he bee-hunted a lot. But I don't believe I ever remember him a-going fishing or hunting, either one.

When he wasn't a-farming, he'd be carpentering. He done all of his work in his big old log shop, about thirty feet long. Well, our house was on a little hill, and his shop building was about two hundred feet due east of that, just above Slate Creek that run south into Spadra [Johnson County, Arkansas]. And the big barn was about the same distance south of the shop. He'd rigged up some pipes so water from the creek would keep a big watering trough for the stock full. He'd made the trough out of a gum log three foot thick and ten foot long that he'd hollowed out.

My daddy would cut down a big straight hickory tree and he'd split it up into squares—quarter it. Then he'd lay it up in that old log shop, to season, dry out. That way, he'd have dry timber there all times of the year. In the spring and early summer, when it was too bad to farm, he was out a-gitting

97

that timber, and making chairs or other things for the house or for farming. He was at home all the time, 'cept when he went off with a load of chairs, or something else he'd made, to sell 'um.

Course, it didn't cost my daddy nothing for timber to make chairs and other furniture out of, but he didn't git no money till he sold 'um.

When he'd git a load of chairs made, he'd put a big frame he'd made up on top of our wagon.

Course, Daddy had a turning lathe for making the parts of a chair. But the bottom would be made out of splits—strips of hickory or white oak wove in and out. That's one of his chairs you're a-setting in now, I guess. I'd imagine it's over eighty year old—and just as steady as it was when he made it.

You don't reckon them chairs made in a factory'll last that long, do ye?

He'd stack them chairs in each other. Them chairs, they had to be folded double: he'd put one up this way, and then he'd put the other one right up the other way, and let the back go right in there, ye see.

And he'd hitch up his best mules to that wagon, and haul them to Clarksville. Yeah, down around Clarksville, and Lamar. That's the next little town. He'd start off with more than a hundred chairs stacked up high, asking everybody everywhere, didn't he want some chairs?

And he sold 'um for . . . I believe he got, it was a dollar and a quarter, or a dollar and a half, apiece, something like that. The best I remember. I don't remember, exactly. That's been seventy years. That wouldn't sound reasonable nowadays, high as everything is. But dollars was dollars then [in 1900].

Well, back then, if folks needed chairs to set on, they might have to make them out of logs—maybe cut out benches or stools with a saw and ax. Some of Dad's old chairs would last fifty or a hundred years; but if a family couldn't afford his, they might have enough money to buy some of these old factory-made cane-bottom chairs. I think they cost about a dollar apiece back then.

But heck, they'd just as soon break all to pieces. Last maybe a year or two.

Selling Chickens on Saturday

FOLKTALE, RELATED ON SEPARATE OCCASIONS
BY ABE KING AND DILLON O. WHITLOW

A good many years ago, I lived up above Clarksville in Johnson County [Arkansas]. And I had a neighbor that run a little store. He wasn't making but just enough money for his family.

One spring, he got the idea to make some extra money. Artificial ice was new there, about two miles from a little railroad station. And so he commenced to buy some ice every Saturday morning. Then he'd put it in a barrel of water. He'd buy him some frying-size chickens; and he'd dress 'um and keep 'um in that cold water till he sold all that he'd dressed.

By the end of July, his business was pretty good, and he was selling about a dozen chickens every Saturday to his customers for Sunday dinner. Course, he had to be careful, for what he dressed and didn't sell, he and his family would have to eat. That was before they had electricity there. No refrigerators.

One Saturday, business at the store was slow. And when it commenced to get about sundown, the old feller—King Ramsey, that was his name—he hadn't sold all his dressed chickens. Then in come a woman who occasionally bought one chicken. Just one, for herself and her husband. Miz Mars.

"Did ye save a chicken for me, King?" she asked.

"I shore 'nuff did," he told her as he reached into the barrel and came up with a middle-sized fryer in his hands. "How's this 'un?"

She eyed it carefully . . . Then she said, "That there 'un's a mite smallish. I'd rather have a bigger 'un."

Old King had had a long day, a hard day. And he was anxious to close up and go home. He pitched that chicken back in the barrel, and reached in, hunting for a larger one. Then he discovered that the one Miz Mars had just looked at and didn't want, that was the only chicken he still had.

Course, old King didn't have to tell her all he knew. He acted like he was a-touching three or four chickens in the barrel. Then he took that same chicken back out of the water. He squeezed it on the bottom to make it look bigger than it was. He held it by the wings, to show her it was strong. Then he says, "How's this one, Miz Mars?"

For a full minute, that little old lady stared at that scrawny bird. At last she said, "I believe I'll take it."

But she kept standing and looking at that chicken.

Finally she says, "My sister, Flossie, may come to see us tomorrow, with her man and kids. I believe I will take 'um both, King."

Accidental Doctor

WILLIAM HENRY EARLY

Wa-a-ay back, we had an old doctor. He didn't have no license to practice medicine, but they wasn't a-bothering him. They just let him go ahead, ye know, and practice. Old Dr. Gideon is who he was.

Well, he was talking to my father about his practice. And he told him, he says, "Whenever I'm called to see a patient, I go in there, and I set down. And I reach down in my pill bags; and the first bottle of medicine I get ahold of, I give that feller some of it."

Now, ain't that a good one?

And my father says to him, he says, "You're a accidental doctor. You might accidentally kill somebody."

But he didn't have nothing in that pill bag that would hurt anybody, I guess.

Well, he'd been doing that for quite some time. Wy, yeah. He'd been messing around long enough that he ought to know something about what would kill anybody. But he didn't have anything that would kill anybody.

They wouldn't allow him to do it, I guess.

Charging for Know-how

REUBEN CAUDLE

I've got a doctor story I can tell ye.

I remember a feller, Bill, that got a thorn in his finger. He went to Dr. Campbell. And the doctor got it out, and charged him a dollar.

Well, Bill didn't say anything. He just paid it.

Some time later, Bill came along. Dr. Campbell had a cow that had just freshened; and he was trying to milk her, and he couldn't milk her.

He asked Bill to help. And Bill milked her.

Then the doctor said, "Well, thank you, Bill."

"Oh, no," said Bill. "You charged me a dollar fer pullin' that splinter out, and I'll have to have a dollar for milkin' that cow."

Convicts Worked in Coal Mines

HORACE MAYNARD WHITE

They worked the prisoners up here in the coal mines. They'd go to the government, and it would lease them out. And the coal operator would bring 'um up here [to Anderson County, Tennessee] and work 'um for nothing.

Course, that would take jobs away from the miners; and they got tired of that. So the miners' association decided, "We'll turn you loose," meaning the prisoners.

And so the old miners got together down here. And they went up through the mining camps. When they got through and come back home, wy, there was no stockade for the prisoners, nothing. They had turned them all loose.

We lived back in the mountains at that time. And the prisoners would pass our place going in that mountain, and going to the New River. Getting away.

And whenever a bunch of 'um would pass, Mother'd have corn bread and bacon fried for them —to give them men, to tide them on their way across that mountain. They'd try to get to the

New River, that runs north, and they could just float down it; or they'd catch a train and get gone there somewhere, if they could get any money for fare. I don't know where they'd go to.

Ye see, my mother's family was miners, the menfolks. And she wanted the prisoners to get away, so there'd be jobs for the miners.

The men was nearly working for nothing, anyhow.

I always got about a dollar and one cent a ton, most of the time, when I worked. I always made good money, mining. After they got rid of the prisoners.

Youth Worked at Barrel-Stave Mill

LEE WERT

I jist played a little ball at school. Then, it wasn't so many black people where we lived. Didn't have enough players for a baseball team. We just had a very small school, and it was open maybe three months in the summer, till fall. Once a year. And I had to work the rest of the year.

My father put me to working on public works for the Greenwell Stave Company in October when I was fourteen in September [in 1904]. And I worked nine years at public works at these little groundhog sawmills and stave mills; and that's the kind of work I done.

If I was to tell you the truth, when he put me in public works, he had a family of four children and mother and father at home. And when I got that little check of mine, I carried it and give it to Father.

And maybe he'd give me a dollar, or a dollar and a half. Course, he fed me and clothed me, and all the other.

And I worked nine years on public works. And I tell the people now that I think I'd be safe in saying that ninety-five dollars out of every hundred I made went to support my father and his family.

Until the last month I worked. I told him—that was in January, I told him in December—I said, "Well now, Dad, I'm goin' to get married on the second of February." I said, "I can't help you-all enny more, because my January work —I'm going to have to have it to marry."

So I married then, and quit public works. And I went to farming. And I farmed right there on that one farm thirty years.

Well, I told him that.

And he just said, "Well, son, you've done a good job for us. We appreciate it."

The Gypsies' Trading Horse

TOM CAUDLE

I remember when my father owned oxen. I wasn't big enough to plow, but I can remember about them. He had one yoke of oxen, some little black steers, and some mules, too. These black oxen would take a turning plow and stay on the same land with these mules. They'd walk as fast pulling a plow as the mules. That was unusual for a yoke of oxen; generally, they were quite a bit slower.

And I recall when I was about, I guess, four years old, some gypsies camped near our home. They always had with them a trained horse that, if you traded for that horse, you couldn't get it away from their camp. Then you'd want to trade back; and they'd pull your leg for five or ten dollars' profit, you know.

Well, my father was a horse trader. And he traded for that bay horse with them gypsies. He knew what he was a-getting when he was a-getting it.

Then he told one of his boys to go get Old Buck and Lett. He didn't send for the little black steers. They were bad to run away, and besides, he wanted his big steers so's he could take that bay horse he'd traded for, whether that horse wanted to go, or not.

Pretty soon, brother Eustice got there with that great big yoke of oxen. Then him and Dad went to putting the chain around this horse's heart girth, and in between his front legs; and they was a-going to tie his head to that log chain that was fastened on the other end to them oxen's yoke.

Them gypsies saw what my father was a-playing—he'd beat them at their own game. The gypsy women went to squawling, and they was a-screaming, "You're about to kill our horse!"

Course, then that horse didn't belong to them gypsies.

And so the head man of them gypsies told Daddy to unchain the horse. He said, "Well, the women, they're having so much fit about that horse, I'll give ye ten dollars if you'll swap back with me."

They'd been figuring on making about ten dollars' profit —making Dad pay that much extra to get his old horse back after he found out his new one wouldn't work for nobody but them gypsies.

Well, my father knew he could take that trick horse away behind them big steers. And then he'd take the ten dollars off of them before he'd agree to trade back.

Course, ten dollars was worth a lot more back about 1892 or '3.

7

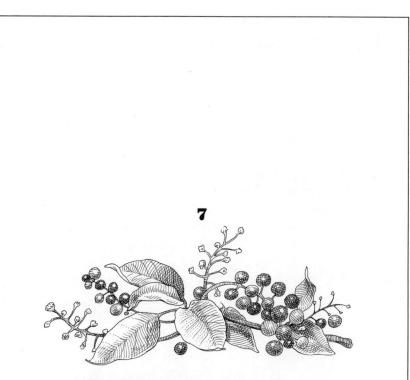

"We had good neighbors"

Neck, Alabama

ULUS S. HUCKABY

My daddy was left a orphan after the Civil War. He was born in 1863, see. And he didn't have no schooling. His mother was a renter on them big farms around Bridgeport [Jackson County, Alabama]. His father never did come home from the Civil War.

And this boy grew up. He went to work when he was six years old. He never had a Santa Claus. He never went to school.

But finally, my daddy got up a pretty good education. I don't know how he got it. He didn't have no children that could teach him. Ma couldn't teach him. He must've read everything he could get his hands on.

So, it was three mile and a half to the post office, in Union Grove, Alabama. And he told Momma one day, he said, "I'm going to write to the government for a post office."

"Wy," she said, "Jim, they won't give you no post office."

But they did.

And he wanted to name it N-I-C-K. He'd bought the land

where he lived from Nick Stephens. He wanted to name it Nick, but on the application he didn't dot his "i."

And they named it Neck, Alabama.

He got the post office. Right in our house, ye know. We had a little plank house, with one little side room. We didn't have to go after our mail.

That place ought to have become a center, a town. About ten miles, every way, they wasn't a post office or nothing.

But the rural route came. Killed it dead as a hammer. Broke its neck.

Neighborliness

DILLON O. WHITLOW

Back when I was young, we had good neighbors. And when somebody in the community needed help, wy, they got it.

Where I was raised, both White and Independence counties [Arkansas]—wy, they was good people. Now, here in White County, Dad owned a farm. But he rented what land he farmed in Independence County. He rented it on the White River. He owned his home.

That was just above Batesville. He owned a home there, in the town. But then we went to the river and rented land. We went down there to farm cotton and corn. That was on the White River I'm talking about.

But in White County, I remember very well. The neighbors then, they had rail fences. They couldn't go to town and buy wire and build them a fence. They had rail fences. And they'd have what they call rail-maulings. We had one. And you'd just cut your timber and get it all ready. And then you'd invite your neighbors all in.

And the women would all come to help cook the big dinner. And they'd cook a big dinner. And the men would split them rails. Well, we went all around. All the neighbors that needed rails would get them made that way.

Well, generally, they would make a feller some rails and lay them out where he wanted to build the fence. That's called "laying the worm." And if they'd made what rails was needed, they might help him put up the whole fence.

But probably they wouldn't do it all the time, lay the fence. I know they didn't in our case. We built the fence after the rail-mauling. They called it a rail-mauling here. In some other places, they'd call it a rail-splitting. It was all the same thing.

And they'd help out one another that way. Hog-killing, would do the same thing. They'd swap work enough that they wouldn't have to pay out any money, your neighbors would.

And they'd swap meat, too. That was common. Give you part of their meat, some fresh pork, for help with hog-killing.

And sometimes they would kill something before cold weather: beef and pork, but mostly pork. One family would kill and divide up with three or four of his neighbors. Then another one would kill, and pay back what he got from you.

Course, back before we had refrigerators, we couldn't keep it long in hot weather. That was about the only way you could do it.

When they'd have a rail-mauling, wy, a lot of times the women would have a quilting at the same place. Uh-huh. And then, maybe they'd have a dance that night.

The Birthday Party

FRED MCCOY

My daddy-in-law was a good old man. He was always a-helping everybody around that needed help; and once in a while, he was trying to help somebody that didn't need no help, or didn't want none, one. He didn't mean no harm, Uncle Reese didn't. Everybody that knowed my wife's daddy called him Uncle Reese.

Well, Uncle Reese was awful particular about nearly everything he done, and what others around him done. He was a feller that seemed like he wanted to boss, and be on the run all the time.

I tell ye: it was plenty hard to figure out how to get along with him sometimes, when he wanted to boss me. I guess all his kinfolks figured I done a better job that way than any of his blood kin.

Well, one time, he had a birthday a-coming up. And we aimed to slip it up on him.

Well, Uncle Reese was the awfulest bee hunter you ever saw in your life.

His kinfolks planned on having a birthday party for the old feller, and not let him know anything about it till noon on a Sunday.

Well, they all knowed I could handle him a little bit, and they knowed me and him was both big bee-tree hunters. And they fixed it up for me to get him off to where they could arrange things that Sunday morning, without him a-knowing about it.

He had some brothers at Jacktown and all around here in Madison and Washington counties [Arkansas]. And it took them all day to drive over here in buggies and ride horses; it took ye nearly to noon to get here.

And they told me to keep him out on this bee hunt till late noon.

Well, we had some little water holes just over the other side of that bluff out yonder, where bees was a-watering. And we'd go out there and take their course—see whichaway they was a-goin' back to their trees. And then we'd take out a-looking for their tree. Me and him found a lot of bee trees thataway, and we generally had honey at our houses.

Well, it come that Sunday morning, and his wife fixed him up the worst rig of clothes [that is, worn, tattered] you ever saw, for him to put on. He'd put on anything. She would tell him, "Over there's the stuff for you to put on," and he'd put it on. But they was clean clothes, they wasn't dirty. They was some patched britches, and a patched shirt.

Early that morning, he told the rest of the family, "Well,

I aim to bee-hunt with Fred today." That's me. He said, "Fred's done cut a bee course."

Well, I'd went over there to that water hole the evening before and blazed some bushes along the way I was going to say I saw some bees go, and lined them up. That's what I'd done. I'd blazed them bushes, hacked them a little with a ax, but I hadn't seen no bees there.

We went over there first thing that morning, after breakfast. And I said, "One of them bees was watering right there." Fact is, wasn't no bees coming there, then nor the day before, neither. I told him, "One would go right through where them bushes is blazed."

"Yeah," he said, "now, did you see them do it?"

And I said, "You bet you." And he knowed I had a good eye for bee-hunting. He knowed I looked them over good.

We hunted on that course till late noon. There never had been a bee went there. I'd follow him along and show him. I had the bushes blazed. Well, we looked the trees up, backwards and forwards.

It's a right smart job to hunt a bee tree. But they was a lot of fun in it, if you like it. In them days, I liked it, and he did, too.

Anyhow, we worked at it there until late noon. And I told him, I said, "It's a little bit after twelve."

And he said, "Let's go to dinner; we'll come back after a little while. We'll find that bee tree."

And I said, "Okay."

I had my folks out there at his house, my wife and children. They had arranged to go out there. Everybody that was a-coming was there at that time. Supposed to be.

We started back. We got along—he was walking fast—to

get a snack of dinner, so we could come back and find that bee tree. And I was walking right behind him. We got along down there, in the pathway.

And the boys opened up with their band, down at his house. It was that Johnson Band of Wesley [Madison County]. And all the boys had their horns there. Prettiest music you ever saw.

Well, when we got to about half a quarter [of a mile] of the house, Uncle Reese heard the music they was a-playing. He turned around to me and he said, "Where is that music?"

I said, "That must be down to Johnson's."

And he said, "It's awful plain," and we went on.

They played loud again, and he said, "That music must be down at our house, that's where they're a-playing."

Well, they was big bushes all around the house where he lived. And sudden, we got to the opening, and there was that big crowd. The preacher was there, and the others—all of his family.

Then he turned to me, and he said, "Did you know they was a-fixing to have this?" And he was a-crying. He'd forgot it was his birthday. He couldn't talk for ever so long. And he just cried.

Well, we'd pulled it. That nearly got me, but it was a joke on him.

He went on down to the house. There was his brothers and their families, and everything, unexpected there. A big dinner.

I had played it on him in a way and manner so sincerely that it was hurting me. And I was lying about it all the time. They was wanting me to do it, and I done it. I worked it on him.

And so everything went off fine. He enjoyed the day, and we did, too. We had a big day, all day of it.

Too Late to Learn

MILES J. WEBB

One time years ago, I was down there at Russellville [Pope County, Arkansas], and I met the Old Man Ferguson. And he said, "Come go with me."

"Whur ye want to go, Mr. Ferguson?"

"A-a-aw, I'm going down to the farm," he said.

So we went almost to Dardanelle, and then turned down the [Arkansas] river. I went down there, and he had a big bunch of tractors plowing cotton. He took me over to his barn and explained how he built that barn. He had a big barn. He showed me all around.

And so, it was getting pretty late. About the time he was starting back, I says, "My granddaddy was buried somewhere in this part of the country. I don't know where, and as far as I know, none of my folks know where."

He says, "I know exactly where he was buried." He says, "The next time you're down here, you come around to me, and I'll bring ye down here and show ye his grave."

Course, I lived in Johnson County. And the next time I went to Russellville, the old man was dead. So I don't know yet where my grandpa was buried. I just put it off too long.

See, he's dead and I'm blind. I reckon none of my family will ever know where he's buried.

A Stubborn Man

FOLKTALE, ANONYMOUS

Uncle Jake Woodley lived somewhere between Clinton and Hector [Arkansas]. And he was a stubborn man who refused to admit that he ever did anything wrong, or ever made a mistake.

One Saturday evening, right after dinner, he rode one of his work mules into town with corn for the miller to grind. And he left the mule with Zack Elder, the blacksmith, and said he wanted Zack to put a full set of shoes on that mule.

Now, Zack was a good blacksmith. It had rained the night before, and several other farmers had come in with work for Zack to do; and they got there ahead of Jake.

Jake was fixing to go fox-hunting that night, so he was in a bit of a hurry to get his mule shod. He commenced watching to see if old Coaly, his mule, had his new shoes on, so he could go on home. For two or three hours, he had been sitting on the whittlers' bench listening, and telling a story once in a while. He wouldn't tell any long stories—he didn't have time for that. The bench was over in front of the store, so

Jake would listen awhile, then go see if his mule was ready, so he could go home.

And about six o'clock, he gave up on that talking, and walked over to the shed just as Zack had finished trimming Jake's mule's front hoof, and fitting the new shoe to it, ready to nail it on. Well, you always shoe a horse's front feet first, nobody knows why.

Now, Zack had heated the shoe to crimson red, moved it around on his anvil with his long-handled tongs and beat it out to fit the mule's hoof. He'd beat it and shaped it, and put it back in the forge to reheat it. "I guess Coaly will be proud of that one," he said.

Then he dipped that hot shoe into a barrel of water he used to cool and temper the metal he'd worked on. And then he tossed the shoe into a pile of sawdust.

Well, Uncle Jake fidgeted for a minute, then he reached down in that sawdust and picked up that still-hot mule shoe with his bare hands. He dropped it right quick. But he was too stubborn to admit to Zack and some others there that he had acted foolishly by picking up that hot shoe.

Well, Zack had been watching out of the corner of his eye. He didn't dare laugh. He didn't want to have to fight old Jake. But it was just too good an opportunity to tease him. And he said, "Jake, you put that mule shoe down awful fast. It wasn't too hot, were it?"

"Shucks, no, it just don't take long to inspect a mule shoe, Zack," is all he said.

Brother Nep's Recitation

MRS. CORA BRAY BUCKNER KARR

When we lived in Kentucky, we went to school. That was before we moved back here to Phelps County [Missouri].

And my brother, Napoleon, he never did like to go to school. He didn't want to study.

Well, we was gonna have a little program on Christmas. The teacher told him, she said, "Well now, Nep, you'll have to get a little recitation to say at the Christmas program." We all called him Nep.

And Nep said, "No, I'm not gonna say nothin'."

She said, "Well, I'll have to punish ye." Her name was Miss Alice Allison.

So I was afraid she'd whip him. Me and Nep was awful close. I wouldn't have had nobody to of whipped him for nothing. And I was scared to death that she was going to punish him, if he didn't get a piece to say.

I said, "Now, brother, you'll have to get a piece to say, because Miss Alice will punish ye if ye don't."

"No," he said, "I ain't goin' to."

I said, "Well, I'll tell you what to say."

He said, "What?"

I said, "Well, when they call your name, you get up there. You walk up on the stage. And you say:

"Oh, Lord, look down on us little scholars;
We have a fool to teach our school,
And pay her forty dollars."

But I didn't think he'd say it.

And so that night at the program, Miz Alice called Nep Bray's name. She said, "Recitation by Nep Bray."

Course, they wore knee pants, an' the little pants buttoned on the waist. He looked awful cute. And he walked right up there on the stage. And he just said what I'd told him to.

I just knowed on Monday, he'd really be beat to death.

But Miz Alice never said a word to him. She just thanked him, because he didn't cause her any trouble.

Aw, we had lots of good times.

8

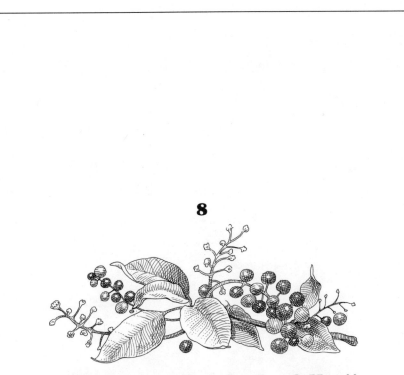

"Every girl of us had a feller"

A Teenager's Flirtations, 1880s

MRS. LIZA ANN CARTER SMITH

We never went to no dances till we was grown, or pretty near it.

We all lived right around the same neighborhood, where we was. And them's the ones we married. We got to know the boys and girls in the other families. My goodness, yes! They was just the same as brothers and sisters, almost, to us.

Yeah, one old boy, he said to me one day, he said, "Hey!" —he called me "cutie" all the time—he says, "Hey, cutie."

I says, "What?"

He says, "Did you ever think you'd be my wife?"

I says, "No. When you was a little 'un, you used to carry on so, I wished a many a time I could just gather you up, and tie you against somethin', and get me a good switch, and wear you out."

"Well," he said, "if you had a' done that, you wouldn't a' had me now."

"Oh," I said, "I wouldn't a' whupped ye that hard." I just laughed.

Oh, Lord, I'm tellin' you right, I'd like to live my life over.

Box Suppers and Pie Suppers

MRS. BELLE BUNCH FANCHER

We used to have pie suppers when I was going with the boys. But sometimes it wasn't just a pie, it would be a big box of food.

And the girls would put fried chicken and everything in it. And it was a box supper, all right. It would be to raise money for the church or the school. The church we went to was to the Liberty United Baptist Church. And the church got the money.

Well, somebody would auction off the boxes. The boys and men would bid on different girls' boxes. And the boys would always manage to find out which was the box they wanted to bid on. They always did. And the boy I went with, he'd find out which box was mine.

A lot of times, when the bidding was for the box of a real popular girl, they'd run the bidding on up. Yeah. They'd always do that. And the church would raise more money that way.

And if it looked like a boy would just keep on bidding, some other boy might try to really run it up on him. But sometimes they'd knock it off on him. Maybe he'd just quit bidding. He might have run out of money, and had to quit bidding.

Course, if a boy took a girl to a box supper and quit

126

bidding on her box—let some other boy buy her box and eat with her—well, that was a risk he had to take. She'd find out that he was too stingy to buy her box. Maybe they'd bid it up to four or five dollars for a real popular girl, and he wouldn't have that kind of money.

If he was just stingy, that's a pretty good way to find out.

Later on, when my daughters took just pies to them, they'd call them pie suppers.

Sidesaddles and Romance

MRS. ROY WARD

Well, I've went to a many a party or dance riding a horse. Course, it was fashionable for girls and women to ride a sidesaddle, if they had one. But lots of families couldn't afford them. And I did ride without a sidesaddle some of the time when I was a girl. Yes sir, I shore did.

And it was thought to be respectable in our neighborhood for women to ride with a regular man's saddle. It was when I was riding. Nearly all the women rode that way.

But back there, yonder, when I was just little, I remember the old sidesaddles. Womenfolks would get on them to go to quilting parties. My brother, before I was old enough to remember, he'd take a horse, and take Mother and my older sisters to the parties, and then come back with them. He'd go three or four or five miles—take them to these quiltings —see that they got there safe. And then he or my daddy would go get them.

The horse we owned when I got up fourteen and fifteen was full of tricks. And Daddy wouldn't let me ride him sideways. He said I couldn't stay on him. He was probably right—he was most of the time.

Well, one time, after I was grown, I went to a ball game, a baseball game, with a girlfriend. And I rode that wild horse of ours. And we came to a lane, a long lane. And my girl-friend suggested we run a race.

Well, I just turned my horse loose; all I had to do was turn mine loose, and tell him to go. He was gone!

Well, the next day, on Sunday, we went to Concord [Cleburne County, Arkansas] to sangin'. And a boy went home with me.

And when we got back to that lane whur my horse had run that race the day before, wy, course my horse was up for another race. And he let out. And he run plum off and left that boy that was with me.

And that boy, he got so mad. He just got mad all over. He thought I did it a-purpose.

I told him I couldn't help it. I couldn't hold him down. I just blistered my hands, a-holding to the bridle—the reins— a-trying to hold him down. But I couldn't. And I even lost my saddle blanket.

Well, a boy—that boy—don't want a girl to outdo him. I just thought, "He's not going to go with me enny more."

But he didn't quit, at all. He got in a good humor. I reckon I convinced him I didn't do it on purpose. Anyhow, he kept going with me, awhile.

A Corn Shucking, Followed by a Square Dance

MRS. LIZA ANN CARTER SMITH

My daddy used to have the awfulest corn shuckings. Oh, Lord, yes. That's what us girls would want. Get a whole lot of them old boys around, shucking corn in the daytime. Yeah. And then, that night, we'd have a little square dance.

Lord! Be a sight to see us kids.

I had my dad to laugh until his stomach hurt him. And he'd have to sit down, laughing at us kids a-dancing.

One big old tall boy used to dance with me, pretty near all the time. They all wanted to dance with me, but some way, he would always get in first. Me and Ken, we used to just tear the floor up, dancing to-gether.

They tried to make me quit dancing with Ken. The other boys wanted me to dance with them. They wanted Dad to make me quit dancing with Ken.

Dad says, "No, I can't do that. I ain't her feller. I can't stop her, or nothing. You let that boy alone. Now, you—plenty more out there—you can get you a girl, if you want one."

"Yes. But I'd rather have her," they'd say; "she can dance better than the others."

Dad said, "Well, you can dance with another one and learn her. She can learn."

Well, after a while, every girl of us had a feller, and dancing to beat the band. Wouldn't nobody trade their feller for another one, just for a dance.

Love at First Sight

MRS. NANCY ANNIE CLINE LUSK

I was born in Tazewell County, old Virginia. And my father moved us to Wyoming County, West Virginia, when I was four. They was eight of us children, and I am the oldest.

I've done all the work they was on a farm, nearly. Cooking, washing dishes, washing clothes, milking, plowing, and chopping.

And I was twenty years old, past. Wasn't married—hadn't thought much about it. I was plain. They called me old Plain Ann, because I wouldn't try to alter myself. I said I was well pleased with my form that God gave me. And I wasn't going to try to alter it, nor my looks neither.

I never went with the boys much. Daddy didn't want me to. I was too good a hand on the farm. I stayed with him until I was twenty-one years old, the only one of the children that done that.

Well, one Sunday I went to church with my father. That was on Brier Creek, an old regular Baptist church. We was going towards the church house door and I saw this man a-standing out. I'd heard of him. But I didn't know then— when I was looking at him there—that he was the one. Big Alver, that's what they called him. He weighed two hundred and two pounds, and it wasn't fat—he was just a large stout man.

And he kept standing there. He wore plain-like clothes. They were neat. He had on a Stetson, black Stetson hat, which he always wore.

We went inside, everybody, for church.

And he behaved nice. He wasn't one of them feisty kind.

But he kept a-looking at me. And my daddy had noticed it. He noticed. And church let out.

And Daddy never had offered to let me ride behind him. He'd ride a horse and I'd walk. But that day, he rode up by a stump, where I could hop on that horse behind him. He said, "Hop on, and let's get home." He said, "Mollie will be a-having dinner ready, a-waiting on us." That's what he called my mother. She was a Lockhart, Mary was her name, but he called her Mollie.

So we got on our way and Daddy said, "I think Big Alver was thinking about asking you to let him walk you home."

Well, a short time later, Mother asked him to call for our mail, and relay it to us. We lived a way off from the post office. And Big Alver had a sawmill set up pretty close to us, to our house.

And he soon got a letter for us, and brought it up.

We got to talking, and went from that.

And the first thing you know, we were just a-getting along fine.

Shivarees

HARRY L. BURNS

Used to, they'd have shivarees in our community. That would be the first night after two people from our community got married. My goodness alive, I reckon we had shivarees! I don't know how they originated. But my! I went to some of the awfulest shivarees that ever was.

Well, the neighbors—mostly young folks—they'd show up where the couple was gonna be right after dark. And they'd make the awfulest noise. They'd beat plow points and sweeps, and things like that—and shoot shotguns, and everything else they had. And they'd make all the racket they could.

Course, the couple would nearly always know ahead of time they was going to be shivareed; and it would always be right after dark, right after they was married. And they'd be a whole bunch of them there in the dark, making all that racket. They'd keep it up till the husband would come out. And then maybe we'd dash a bucket of water on him.

Sometimes the couple would come out and invite everybody in for refreshments. Sometimes they would . . . and sometimes they wouldn't. And sometimes they would never come out.

They shivareed me. My gosh! That's coming on seventy years ago.

Course, I expected them to shivaree us—we expected it. Now, if they hadn't come and shivareed us, I'd have been disappointed. Yes, I sure would.

Small Houses

MRS. PEARL THOMAS WILLIAMS

In the early days, lots of families wouldn't have but two or three rooms in their homes. And one room would have a fireplace. That's where the family would stay in cold weather, till they got ready to go to bed.

And when a boy would go to court his girl, wy, they didn't want to stay in the livin' room with the rest of the folks.

So they'd build a fire in the cookstove in the kitchen, if they had a cookstove.

And I've heard a girl that was a little older than me, Mary Kelly, tell about how she and her beau, Henry Grissom, would go in the kitchen in cold weather so they could talk. Mary said, "We done purt' near all our courtin' over the cookstove, along."

Well, she and Henry finally got married.

Flowers and Plums

MRS. SARAH BOWEN BURNS

My husband loved flowers so good. And I raised lots of them, for him. And I keep them at his grave. He's been dead about fifteen years.

Well, I raised sunflowers and moss roses and Easter flowers. Yeah, that's the kind I'd raise. We'd have a row clear around our house. And they'd make boxes around . . . to put flowers in.

One time I set out a plum tree, an' named it. I named it for a boy I was a-going with. Yeah.

And it bore plenty. I never saw th' like of plums.

I dragged that tree a right smart piece. And I set it out, when I lived out there . . . stayed out there with my daddy and momma.

And, oh! You want to know what I named it? Roland Davis. He came to ask for me twice. And I wouldn't have him . . . after I named that bush after him.

I turned him down. But I had plenty of plums, though.

9

"They preached the Bible"

The Preacher Who Lost His Sermon

OSCAR UNDERWOOD

Well, my folks was Baptists. My father and mother was Baptists, and I was a Baptist. And we had an o-o-old preacher, just a real old feller, preached at our church when I was a boy. And he'd tell his stories about when he was a boy, and when he started out, commenced a-preaching.

He said he started out pretty tol'ble young, a-preaching in an old log house. They built an old log house, for a church. And he said they bored some holes back in the logs, right behind where he stood, you know, and preached.

He said he started out a-writing out his sermons. And he'd roll that sermon up and put it back in one of them auger holes, so if he kinda forgot part of it, he'd reach back of him and pull it out of that auger hole. And could just go right ahead, and people would not know the

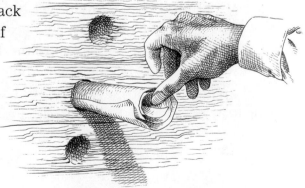

difference—wouldn't know he forgot part of his sermon.

Well, one Sunday morning, he forgot part of what he wanted to say, and he reached back there to get his sermon. And he pushed it back further in the auger hole. And he kept a-trying to get it. And every time he would push it back a little further, into that auger hole.

Then he got more interested in that auger hole than he was in what he was a-saying. He forgot his sermon, and couldn't think of nothin' to say.

Then he just stopped and said, "Well, folks, I've got a good sermon back here in this auger hole. But I've got it pushed back where I can't get it."

Preacher Johnny Crisp

EDWARD CULLER

My mother liked good singing. You know that I can remember when I was a young feller, seeing my mother profess and join the church. And I seen one brother and three sisters profess and join the same church—all of them baptized in a little old creek, when I was a young feller.

My brother that's a-livin' yet has been a deacon of that same church for over sixty-five years. Baptist church. And we had a Methodist church around then, too.

And we had one preacher, one that preached at our church. They said he was pretty bad on the Methodists, a feller Crisp, Uncle Johnny Crisp. I can remember him. They said he was pretty tough—he didn't believe in the Methodist, much.

Most of the preachers way back, you couldn't hardly tell whether they was Baptist or Methodist. Oh, yeah. We used to mix up. We didn't pay much attention to which was which —that's right.

When the Methodists had a meeting this side of Remable [Watauga County, North Carolina] the Baptists went there. When the Baptists had a revival and the Methodists didn't have one, wy, the Methodists come there, a lot of them.

Course, if a preacher jumped on the other ones, they wouldn't come to hear him much. But some of them would, anyhow.

One time, Preacher Johnny Crisp was preaching up here at Cold Spring. And during the service, wy, people were getting up and going out, ye know, occasionally.

This old man Crisp, he just didn't like that at all. I know that he didn't. I didn't hear him—I wasn't there. But it was the Cold Spring church. Miz Leal Winkler told me. She said she was there, now, and she heard it.

Well, these two young fellers got up and started out. And Crisp, he just quit preaching till they got outside. And when they got gone, wy, he started right back where he quit off at.

And a short time later, wy, one or two more got up and started out. But before they got out of the door, she said the old man said, "Boys, just go on to hell, where you started."

One of them boys turned around and said, "What do you want me to tell the Devil when I get there?"

Well, Miz Winkler said Crisp just walked down out of the

pulpit, and shook his finger at them, and said, "Tell the Devil I'm a-sendin' him two more pups!" Yes sir. He said, "Tell the Devil I'm a-sending him two more pups."

A Surprise Dinner Guest

MRS. MARGARET MOFFITT HOKE

My mother said that when they'd go to a preaching, churches was far apart. Sometimes you'd have a way to ride or walk.

One Sunday, the service was over and the preacher was wanting to go home for dinner with some of 'um. And nobody didn't invite him.

So then my grandmother told him, she said, "You can go home with me. We're not expecting company. But you're welcome to what we have."

My mother was just a girl. And she ran on ahead, to home, ahead to her grandmother. The preacher was a-coming! And she told her grandmother—her name was Agnes, but everybody called her Aggie—she said, "Grandma Aggie, Mother's invited the preacher to come home for dinner."

And her Grandma Aggie said, "That's all right. What I've got, I didn't know we was gonna have company."

And then she said, "What I've got, if he's a good man, it's good enough for him. And if he's not, it's too good."

Two Sons Enter the Ministry

MRS. PEARL GARLAND

Well, in this community, they didn't have their own preacher. There'd be one come in like the first Sunday of each month and preach, or some other Sunday each month.

One Sunday, after the morning sermon, the preacher went to the old farmer's house for dinner. The farmer didn't know the preacher was comin' home with 'um, and they didn't have much fixed to eat.

So his wife told her husband to go out and kill a couple of roosters for dinner. He went out and killed two young roosters, and she fried them.

And a little after noon, they set down to dinner. And the preacher ate most of the chicken. They didn't have very much else on the dinner table to eat.

And there were some boys in that family. But they didn't get much of that chicken. And them two biggest boys, they just kept a-staring at the preacher, watchin' him eat.

After they got through eating dinner and set and talked awhile, wy, the farmer took the preacher out and was showing him over his place. And nearly ever'where they went, there was this old rooster, just keeping on crowin', big and loud.

Dreckly, the preacher said, "That rooster seems mighty proud of himself."

And the farmer said, "Well, he should. He just had two sons to enter the ministry."

Funeral Sermon Weeks after Burial

MRS. NANCY ANNIE CLINE LUSK

We didn't have a preacher in our community when I was little. They'd bury people right after they died, but they'd have to wait until a preacher came to have a funeral service —weeks or months later, in the wintertime.

The first one I can remember that I went to, I was about six years old. They were preaching funerals out in a grove.

And they had split little poplar trees, and made seats— had legs on 'um. Made seats.

And they had a all-day meeting. That time, a preacher preached six different funerals.

Like I said, people used to bury the dead, and maybe it would be a lo-o-ong time before they'd ever preach the funeral. And he preached six different sermons that day.

I know. I was just barely big enough to go to church. Well, their heads was all bowed. Bowed with their handkerchiefs to their faces. And I didn't see nothing to cry about. But I thought I should act like that. So I played like I was crying. I put my handkerchief to my eyes.

I didn't know what a funeral was. They'd talk about it at home, but I didn't know enough to understand.

It was a Baptist preacher. Yeah, it was a long time before I ever went to a Methodist church. I belong to the Methodist church now. That's where my membership is, in McDowell County, West Virginia.

Well, they preach the Bible, both of them do. The Methodists tell you, "Sprinkle, if ye want to be." But I believe with the Baptists in going down in the water. I was baptized by immersion.

We used to have a circuit preacher that rode around through the country. But in the towns—like Oceana and Bluefield, places like that—they had regular churches.

And finally, they got to preaching at the schoolhouse.

Something Good to Say about Everybody

MRS. PEARL THOMAS WILLIAMS

When we were at a funeral at Morganton [Van Buren County, Arkansas] not long ago, I was trying to remember how they would conduct funeral services when I was a little girl. Now, I don't know that it was so much different. We never had a choir, never had a solo sung.

But the minister always would tell something about the person, if he had something good that he could tell. If he didn't know much about the deceased, he'd mostly read from the Bible. There's nobody so bad that you can't think of something good to say about him or her.

But I know one time, my husband was down at the post office at Quitman [Cleburne County]. And there was a feller who hadn't lived there so awful long. Everybody liked him. But he was one of these men, just seemed good-for-nothin'. He didn't do much good, or he didn't do any much bad.

And someone said, "Well, that fellow is not good for a thang in this world, I guess."

And someone else that was a-setting there said, "Well now, he's sure a good whistler."

So, there's some good in everybody.

Retribution: Knot on a Fiddler's Thumb

MRS. NANCY ANNIE CLINE LUSK

Our Great-grandpa Henry Cline—Granddad, we always called him—he played the fiddle. He played for entertainment, a long time ago.

And he had a great big knot growed around one of his thumbs. He'd show us, when we were little. He'd come to our house.

And he'd talk to us about how to do to be true to our word. He'd tell us to never lie to God.

Well, the thumb that had that big knot on it, that was the one that he tromped his fiddle string with while he was playing it.

And in his old days, he'd set with his hands up—show us

144

how he used to hold the fiddle. One time long ago, he had a sick child, he said. And he told us how he had lied to God, and that was the cause of that knot on his thumb.

He said he had a great big silk bag of a thing. He said he always tied his fiddle up in that, and hung it onto the wall when he wasn't a-playing.

He said he knowed the child was sick, their baby. But he didn't know it was bad sick. He was playing the fiddle on the front porch.

And his wife took the baby and laid it in his lap. And he didn't even stop playing. He was sitting there plucking on the strings, and he just let the baby lay there—didn't pay no attention to it.

And he said his wife told him he had to take care of the baby—she was going to milk the cow. But he went on, out on the porch, sawing his fiddle.

When she come in, that baby was dead.

"You see," he told us, "I was just so hurt that I just tied that violin up in that silk bag, laid it in the fire, and burnt it." And he vowed that he'd never play again.

"Well," he said, "years went by. And I got over having to give the baby up."

And he finally got to wanting to play the fiddle again. And he went and bought him one. But now he had a knot on his thumb, and he couldn't play the fiddle like he used to.

"You see, there's the knot," he'd say. "That's the way I done it. God set that knot on my thumb. And I couldn't play the fiddle no more."

Yeah, he'd tell us about it. How that it was, to promise God something, and not obey.

We was jist little tots. And he was so wicked.

That's been more than ninety years ago.

10

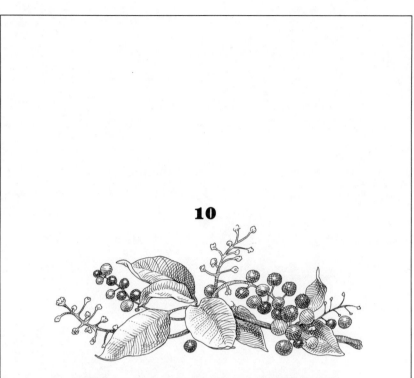

"The war was just pitiful"

Gish's Mill and the Miller

GEORGE CADD

I was raised in the Gish's Mill community [Roanoke County, Virginia]. And that's where I raised my family.

Well, the Gish's mill was built on the Roanoke River, way, way before the Civil War. It used water power, and it ground corn and wheat into meal and flour.

When the Civil War come on, there was a feller named Isaac Vineyard had that mill and was running it. Ike Vineyard. Nearly all the folks around here was for the South; and nearly all the able-bodied men between seventeen and forty-five joined the Confederate Army.

Ike Vineyard tried to keep anybody from knowing it, but he supported the North in different ways. And he'd manage to have a supply of corn and wheat ready to give to the Union Army when it come through.

Before that war, the miller would take one-eighth of the grain his customers brought to him, and he'd grind the rest for them.

During that war, with nearly all the men gone away, Ike

149

commenced to take more and more of their grain for toll. And when he found out he could get away with that— keeping the corn and wheat to give to the Union Army—wy, he'd take nearly all the women brought to him. He'd take nearly everything they had, and give them maybe a gallon of meal for a bushel of grain. Flour or meal. He'd tell them, "That's all ye git. All ye git!"

And Ike Vineyard got by with it, was getting by with it. Well, the women got to talking about what he was a-doing to them, how he was treating them. And they didn't like it a bit.

And they just all got together, and says, "We'll go down there and give him a good whipping."

So, one time, they was eight or ten ladies went down there, and taken Ike Vineyard out there and whipped him, like you was whipping a horse for kicking a cow in the face. They set his old back a-fire.

And then they went in there and took I don't know how much stuff from his mill. They always told me, "We took a lot of that meal and flour out of there."

My grandmother was a-telling me about that. She was one of them eight or ten ladies that went down there and whipped Ike. She said they put an end to the way old Ike was a-cheating them.

And I remember that old dude, Ike Vineyard. He wasn't operating that mill when I can remember, but he still lived in that community.

Futrell and His Ferry

JOE FUTRELL

My grandfather came from Ireland. Futrell is an Irish name. And they come to Tennessee. And he stayed right there until he was thirty-six year old. And then he come right here and settled right down here on this place [Theodosia, Ozark County, Missouri].

Was my grandfather in the Civil War? Let me tell ye . . .

No. I said no. And I'll say yes. They—neither side wouldn't have him, not the Union nor the Confederates.

I'll tell ye what: he was running a ferryboat, and he was on the Tennessee River. And they said that he could do them more good by running backwards and forwards across that river than he could a-being on either side. Neither side wouldn't have him. They said they wanted him to put them over when they arrived.

Yeah, both sides wanted him to run that ferry. Both sides. Both said, "We want him to put us 'cross here . . . and we want him to put us across when we come." He had to be there.

Yeah, he had a big boat, and he could just—about two or three loads—he could take the whole big army across. He

could haul two wagons
and six steers across
at one time. I've
been there . . .
Well, I don't
know whether I
was right where he
was, or not. But it was
right where the Tennessee River crossed from Tennessee
into Kentucky. He said his ferry was right on the state line.

Well, it was slave time, and then the war ended. And he
came to Missouri.

Salt Shortage

MRS. LULA HARRIS GUTHREY

I've heard 'um talk a whole lot about that Civil War. It was
just pitiful for everybody back then. It certainly was.

The old home guards would come home, hunting for men
that shunned out and were lying out [that is, avoiding military service]. They'd run their bayonets through featherbeds
—thinking some menfolks was in the bed, ye know. And
they'd go into the pore old women's fields, and git what little
corn they'd have. And take their cows off and kill 'um.

Wy, it was just a sight on earth how they'd have to do to
stay alive. Course, they just nearly starved. Yes, they just
had to make the best way they could.

My mother was born in 1862, right in the middle of the war. And they all had a time.

For one thing, they didn't have salt to go in their bread. So they'd go in their smokehouse where they'd salted their meat and hung it up. They'd dig up that dirt on the floor and boil it down, and pour the water off, to git a little salt.

I've heard them say that. It was a bad way to git a little salt in their bread. But I reckon they'd have done most anything to git a little salt. For I think you git sick without it, and I think you can die, if you didn't have any salt.

Bitterness after the Civil War

EDWARD LIVINGSTON MILLER

My grandfather was on the Union side in the Civil War. And Uncle George Russell was on the Southern side. Brother-in-laws, now—the very best of friends before that war.

And I've heard my grandfather tell about it lots. After the Civil War, wy, everybody carried revolvers in their belts.

And they were working together one day. And there was something said about the Civil War. And just the minute they said something about the war, each was out with his revolver. And Grandfather said it seemed like half an hour. But he said he guessed they stood there five minutes, anyway, their revolvers on one another.

I don't know whether it was Granddad or Uncle George

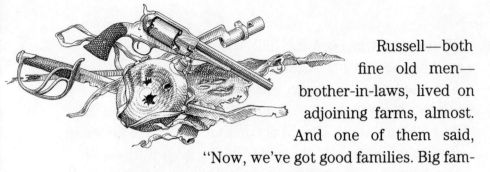

Russell—both fine old men— brother-in-laws, lived on adjoining farms, almost. And one of them said, "Now, we've got good families. Big families." And he said, "Here we stand!"

The other said, "I think I've got the drop on you, and you think you've got the drop on me. We could both pull the trigger at the same time; and there would be two families of orphans."

And the first one said, "Let's put our guns back in the scabbards and never mention that war as long as we live."

Granddad said they shook hands and made a pledge that they'd never mention that Civil War in one another's presence. And they never did as long as they lived.

Now, that took forgiving, did you know!

A Southerner Who Did Not Believe in Confederate Cause

MRS. LULA HARRIS GUTHREY

There was a Mr. Stephenson hid out in a cave during the Civil War. He lived in the South with his family, but he wouldn't fight to help keep slavery.

Well, he'd come out at night. And he was married to my

Aunt Louiza, Grandfather's sister. And he'd come out and hoe in the gardens and crops, when it was dark.

And he and Aunt Louiza had nine boys. I can't 'call his first name right now, but anyway, he was a Stephenson.

And this uncle, he would hide out not far from their house. They had a farm over here, just a little ways. Yes, he'd hide out all day; and Aunt Louizy would work the farm and raise sheep and hogs and cows. And hoe.

And she said he'd go back every morning to that cave. And he would hoe on a moonlight night—he'd hoe row after row.

Some of the family would take him food. And he got all the way through that war without any of his neighbors knowing. But he wasn't thought much of, after that war ended.

I never did know him. He died right after that war ended, and left Aunt Louizy with them nine boys to raise.

Auction of Slaves

THOMAS B. NORMAN

I don't like to hear children crying, yet, after listening to my dad tell this story . . .

My father and his brother, Sam, was about eleven and twelve when the Civil War commenced. And they was orphans. So the county was gonna get them a family—they was going to be bound out. Course, they was white boys.

Well, they took them to a slave market—everything had

to be done legal. And Dad said he had laid there under shade trees on what he called the stock ground, where they'd have these auctions. They took him and Uncle Sam, 'cause they'd have to be wrote up, ye know—to be bound out—have to have papers fixed. They couldn't sell Dad and Uncle Sam. But they was just about like slaves. They was under the hammer, and they was under control—they had them under guard.

And he said they had these three stock pens—he called them—just like livestock pens.

And he said, "I've seen a family of people come in together: a black man and his wife and their children. I seen six children—a man and his wife and six children come in —and get put in a pen.

"Then, when it come sale time, they put the man on the block, and sold him just like a fattening steer. And a man bought him.

"And then they put the woman on, and sold her, and another man bought her who lived the distance of five hundred miles apart from the first man."

That's the way he put it so we'd understand.

"Then," he said, "they put the children on, and sold every one of them. And different men bought them. And each one of them went to a different part of the country, just like the man and woman.

"And when they got the sale over, and they started to gathering up what they'd bought," he said, "I never saw such a struggle in my life . . . I never saw the like. They clinched each other. You could hear them screaming for no telling how far. They had to pull them apart.

"And they took that man, that woman, and them children

away. I don't have the least idea they ever seen one another again, in their life."

I always asked, "What did they do to you and Uncle Sam, Pa?"

He said, "They didn't sell us. But they put us up on the same block. And a man come up and put in his application—what he had to —to git us, according to law, for us to be bound to him to a certain age. He took us several hundred miles to his farm, over the river."

But they got away. They got away from him after that, and come back to whur they'd lived [in east Tennessee]. But they stayed a long time, till they saw the Civil War was ending.

Now, that was terrible.

Note: Long ago, orphans were given court-approved foster parents who would provide a home and care for them to age eighteen—they were bound out.

11

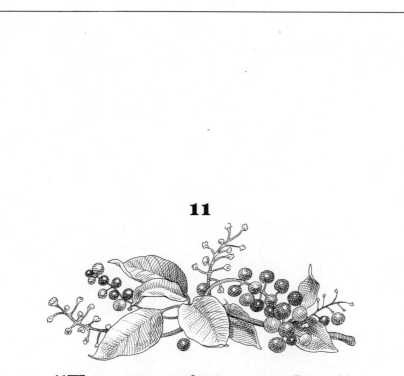

"They was going somewhere"

Great-grandfather at the Toll Bridge

MRS. NANCY ANNIE CLINE LUSK

We was just little tots when Great-grandfather stayed with us one winter.

Now, I'm going to tell ye about his trip—the last trip he ever made—goin' from one of his sons to some more of his family. He was wa-a-ay old then.

He'd loaded up his load on his back. And he started off to—I believe it was off to the ones that he stayed with most.

They'd put in a toll bridge over there, from Charleston out in the mountains, south [in West Virginia]. And they told him he'd have to pay five cents to cross the river on that bridge.

And he would not pay! They were going to charge him five cents.

He took his load off his back, and rolled his pants up. Pulled his shoes off—well, boots. He throwed them across his shoulder, and waded that river. That was out in Raleigh County, to come to Clay County, over the Rockcastle creek.

He said, "Blast your old bridge! I'll just walk!"

That was about 1890 or '91.

A Family Moves in a Snowstorm

FRANK WHITLEY

I was born at Norwood, Wright County, Missouri, in 1894. We were the last black family to move away from there. We moved because there was no school at Norwood. There was eight of we kids, and we were without any school until 1899.

My dad finally was convinced that he had to move. At first, I guess they sort of rationalized. But they finally decided, "Well, we've got to do something."

So we moved down here to Hartville. My dad sold out up there, and bought a little place here on Clark's Creek. That's over here, about four miles from here.

When we moved, we moved on Christmas Eve, 1899. And my feet, and my younger brother's feet, froze as stiff as a stick by the time we got down here. We drove all day in a gale, about twelve miles.

They'd heated up a big boulder, and wrapped it in a gunnysack, and put it in the wagon bed. We kept our feet on that. But before the day was gone, it had turned colder.

When we got here to our new house, my older brother went out and scooped up a tubful of snow. Inside, it began to melt. And Mother set us by it, with our feet in that tub of cold water. And she rubbed them until they thawed out.

That's what saved our feet.

And after coming down here, we got into the school here, and got acquainted with the black people. I had never seen any other black people before. I was five years old then.

You see, in the horse-and-buggy days, then, it would take ye all day with your horse, to go from here to Norwood, about twelve miles, Hartville to Norwood.

Voteless Indians Conscripted for Military Service

MRS. EVELYN MCINTOSH HYATT

They treated the Indians bad in this country . . . they did from the start and they still are. The government, I'm talking about.

Take World War I, for instance. The Indians were not allowed to vote.

And I watched a train as it passed through Waynesville, North Caroline, with a long banner that said: CHEROKEE TRIBE, CHEROKEE, NORTH CAROLINA.

And all those boys in the U.S. Army. To think that they were going to fight for a country, and they were not allowed to vote.

Oh! I tell you: this United States is gonna have to answer for the way they treated the Indians.

If somebody came in and told you to get out of your home and they were going to move in, you'd fight, wouldn't you?

Well, that's what our government did to the Indians.

Trip to California

HIGE BOLES

When I was twenty-four, I went out to California from east Tennessee. I had to ride a train. And I was on the trip nine days a-going. A fifty-five dollar ticket it cost me to go out there. Fifty-five dollars. In 1906.

I had a brother out there. Later, he got a knee hurt and died of blood poisoning. Afore then I went out to see him and look over the country.

You know, by traveling when you're young, you will learn more about the world than anything.

I went out there. I stayed in Placerville—that's where they first discovered gold, ye know. I stayed there for a month or two, in Placerville. That's where my brother died at.

And they just washed that town away, with water, ye know, a-washing to get the gold. They'd been washing it right there more than fifty years. That's where they first discovered gold in California. O-o-oh, yes.

Well, they was old men there who'd been there since 1849. They was old men in 1906, still working. They'd work a little while and get what they call a grub stake. They'd get a donkey and go back in the mountains, and prospect for gold, and stay out there as long as their grub would last. And some would find gold—once in a while, one would do it.

I left that gold camp.

And later on, I was way up on a mountain, in a lumber camp. I was a-rooming with a Frenchman. He had built him a cabin—they had cabins built for us—four men to a cabin. And this Frenchman, he dug him a bathtub out of a log with an adz. And he wanted me to room with him.

And we just had two bunks in his house.

I was just a boy, but he was a kind of a aged fellow then. I remember one morning there, as we come out to work, he said, "We just had a bad earthquake."

And I didn't know nothing about earthquakes—I didn't pay him no attention. We were sixty-five miles back in the mountains. And he said, "We will hear about it in just a little bit."

Sure enough, we got the news that San Francisco was a-burning up. And a lot of the boys—there was no way of getting down to there except by stagecoach—and a lot of the boys left and went to San Francisco to see the big fire.

They like to of never got back. They got into what they call martial law. The army would work 'um here awhile and turn 'um loose. They'd walk on up the street, and the army would work 'um there awhile and turn 'um loose. And they'd just keep 'um running. They like to of never got back.

Later on, after my brother died, I come down to see San Francisco. That place was burnt up as far as you could see. From the middle of town, up Market Street, just as far as you could see, that town was burnt up.

There was one building—the United States Mint—it didn't seem to be touched. A whole lot of big buildings, stone buildings—the whole sides was dropped out of them.

I made three trips out there, to California, all of them more than sixty years ago.

A Man and His Two Motherless Sons

MRS. CORA BRAY BUCKNER KARR

I know one time, we was just all little kids. And they come a man and two little boys. And they was a-foot. They was going somewhere to see if he could find work. And they had buried his wife on the way. In 1902.

They stopped at our house. Mother fixed their dinner. Course, we didn't have too much food then. Our father had died.

And the man said, "Missus, I don't have no money to pay for food."

Mother said, "You don't need no money to have dinner with us." She said, "I was getting dinner, and you're welcome to eat. We don't live high, but we have plenty to eat, what we want."

Course, she had stuff canned in glass jars, and stuff dried, to eat.

And one little boy—we was sitting out in the yard, us kids and them two little boys—and they was telling us about burying their momma, on the road. The oldest one said, "She got sick and died, on the road. We had to bury her and leave her by the side of the road."

Us kids thought that was terrible. We didn't see how anybody could do that.

But there was no other way.

And that man was real—the best I can remember—he was such a humble guy. He was a little frail-looking man. And I think he had tuberculosis.

And I said, "Do you have any money?" to one of the little boys. I was about twelve or thirteen, and the boys, I guess, were about eight and ten.

He said, "Uh-uh. I never did have no money."

I said, "I've got some. I'll give it to you." I just had two pennies.

But I ran in the house and got them pennies, and gave them to him.

Wy, I was so happy! Because he didn't have no money, and I had two pennies. After they left, I told my mother, "Momma, I gave that little boy my pennies."

She said, "Well, honey, in the sight of God, that's just as much as a thousand dollars. It's all you had."

That made me feel better, you know. I thought, now, I had done a good deed.

I'm satisfied that little boy never forgot that. No, he never. And I never did.

It seems like, sometimes, I'd just think, Oh, if I knew where he was, I'd send him some money.

Course, he was a grown man by then. But he always stayed the same, he always stayed little in my sight.

I never did know; we never did hear from the family. And the father he'd kind of promised Mother he would write back, when he got to his destination. But he never did. I guess the poor guy didn't have anything to do it with.

Or maybe he couldn't write. For all I know, he couldn't.

I don't know where they were from. I don't remember that. But they was sure a pitiful-looking sight.

A Centenarian
Talks about Her Father

MRS. EMMA WEAVER BISSETT

My father was the second white child born in Springfield, Missouri, in 1830. But I grew up over west of Springfield, in Lawrence County. And we didn't move back here until I was about seventeen.

My father was gone from Missouri for a long time. First, he volunteered as a soldier in the Missouri Guard, and went off and fought in the War with Mexico. A lot of his friends who went with him from Springfield didn't come back—they were killed in battle. He went down there in 1847.

And after he got back, lots of people here got the gold fever. And he went overland to California, with several people he knew.

The next year, wy, he came back and got his family and took them to California. And they stayed there until 1867. And Father married my mother after his first wife died.

And, in all, Father went to California three times. I think it was the third time he went out there, he went down to Panama on a boat, then  crossed the Isthmus of Panama some way or other. Then he got another ship to San Francisco. The other times, he went overland, riding his own horse, or riding in a wagon.

I didn't listen to him as much as I should. I had music and painting and dances and boys on my mind too much for that. But I remember one little story to tell you.

When they were crossing Panama, they had some kind of meat for dinner that was oh, so delicious. Everybody who ate any of it just raved about it.

And somebody asked what it was.

The waiter said to Father, who spoke Spanish, that it was young monkey.

And they were afraid to tell any of the women—there were several women on that ship. I don't know, but I guess they were wives and fiancées going out to join their husbands in California, or to get married.

I don't remember how he said they got across the Isthmus.

But they didn't tell the women that they'd been eating monkey. They thought that was too much for them to accept.

Epilogue

A Woman, 104, Reflects on Her Long Life

MRS. MAGGIE GRAHAM BRADFORD

I just don't know what changes I would make in my life. But I might correct some mistakes I made. I don't know what they were, but I guess I made some. Everybody else makes them.

When I married, I said I wanted to be a hundred years old, and I wanted to be the mother of twelve children. Now, I made that talk.

Well, I raised eleven of my own; and one stepson made the twelfth.

My grandmother was the mother of twelve. I wanted to be like my grandmother. She lived to be ninety-nine and nine months and a few days, old. But she didn't get her hundred.

I'm the oldest one of the whole generation, I reckon.

And . . . to explain how I got to be as old as I am, I count it willpower. You got to have willpower to do anything, and go through with anything. That's all I can call.

Yeah, and helping the other feller.

I guess I've helped the other feller about as much as any one person that I know of. Not boasting, a'tall.

Notes on the Storytellers

EZRA ADDINGTON, *of Nickelsville, Scott County, Virginia, was born October 20, 1883, and related his story August 8, 1975, in his ninety-second year. He was a public school teacher. He and his wife lived in a large ancestral home well over a hundred years old. ("Preserving Sausage")*

MISS MARTHA (MARSE) AYERS, *a lifelong resident of Formosa, Van Buren County, Arkansas. She was born in 1876 and related her story October 13, 1970. When she was interviewed, she had never tasted a carbonated beverage from a bottle, and had never been outside the state of Arkansas. ("Making Lye Soap")*

A man named BEALE, *other information lacking, related the folktale "Uncle Mary."*

MRS. EMMA WEAVER BISSETT *grew up in rural Lawrence County, Missouri, but moved to Springfield with her parents, married a lawyer, and became a civic leader. She was born September 3, 1872, and related her story June 20, 1973, in her 101st year. ("A Centenarian Talks about Her Father")*

HIGE BOLES, *of Albany, Clinton County, Kentucky, was a former county sheriff and an active licensed real estate agent at the age of ninety-one years. He was born March 19, 1882, and related his story June 24, 1973. ("Trip to California")*

MRS. LOU BOYD *lived at Rumley, Searcy County, Arkansas, and was the wife of a farmer. She was born June 28, 1877, and told her story August 8, 1972. ("A Girl Stays Home")*

MRS. MARGARET (MAGGIE) GRAHAM BRADFORD *lived and raised her own eleven children and one stepchild at Eglantine, Van Buren County, Arkansas. She was born in eastern Kentucky July 13, 1874, and related her story September 29, 1978, in her 105th year. She lived past her 107th birthday. One of Mrs. Bradford's*

177

sons, Everett, was an eighth-grade teacher of Roy E. Thomas at Morganton, Arkansas. ("A Woman, 104, Reflects on Her Long Life")

HARRY L. BURNS *lived at Springfield, Conway County, Arkansas. He was born in 1884 and related his story September 25, 1970. As a young man, he sustained a permanent leg injury when a mule kicked him. He became a pharmacist. ("Shivarees")*

MRS. SARAH BOWEN BURNS *grew up in the Twisting Sourwood community and never left Clay County, Kentucky. She was born April 1, 1875, and related her story a few weeks after her 100th birthday, in June 1975. Her husband was a farmer. ("Flowers and Plums")*

MRS. BETTY ROGERS BYRD *lived at Beebe, White County, Arkansas, and was the wife of a farmer. She was born November 19, 1875, and was interviewed April 14, 1971. ("Goat for a Neighbor" and "Cooking Coon")*

GEORGE CADD, *as explained in his story, lived in the Gish's Mill community, Roanoke County, Virginia, now called Vinton. He was born September 24, 1884, and related his story May 21, 1976. ("Gish's Mill and the Miller")*

JAMES LACK CASE *lived in the South Pittsburg community, Marion County, Tennessee. He was an outdoorsman with few equals, the son of an outstanding marksman. His career was with a cement plant near his home, and he hunted in his spare time, summer and winter, day and night. He was born March 1, 1891, and related his story June 18, 1979. ("Hunting from a Young Age")*

REUBEN CAUDLE, *reared at Scottsville, Pope County, Arkansas, was born in 1882 and related his story September 11, 1970. He was a schoolteacher and taught math at what is now Arkansas Tech*

University, Russellville, Arkansas. He and Tom Caudle were brothers. ("Charging for Know-how")

THOMAS (TOM) CAUDLE *was born in 1888 in Scottsville, Arkansas, and also related his story September 11, 1970, along with his brother, Reuben. He was a farmer for nearly seventy years. ("The Gypsies' Trading Horse")*

CLIFTON CLOWERS *lived on Woolverton Mountain, Conway County, Arkansas, except while serving in the U.S. Army in Europe during World War I. He was born October 30, 1891, and his story was recorded in November 1991, a few days after his 100th birthday. Mr. Clowers has been memorialized in the popular song "Woolverton Mountain," recorded by Nat King Cole and others. That song was written by his nephew Merle Kilgore, a prominent member of the country music community in Nashville. ("The Fight: Coon and Dog")*

MRS. JOHNIE GARDNER CRAIG *grew up at Philadelphia, Izard County, Arkansas, where her father, a college graduate, was the schoolmaster. She was born December 20, 1876, and related her stories October 21, 1980, a few weeks before her 104th birthday. She was a college graduate, and a schoolteacher until her late marriage to a Methodist minister, the Reverend L. C. Craig. One of her sisters also lived to age 100 years. (" 'Our House' " and "Mother's Two Annual Trips to Town, to Shop")*

EDWARD CULLER *was a lifelong resident of Boone, Watauga County, North Carolina. His life's work was as an employee of what is now Appalachian State University, starting shortly after it was founded. He lived within walking distance of his job and never owned an automobile. He was born November 11, 1890, and related his story October 13, 1974. ("Preacher Johnny Crisp")*

MARION L. (DOC) DAVIS, *reared by Hurricane Creek, southern Newton County, Arkansas, was born January 10, 1870, and related his story September 24, 1970, in his 101st year. He was a successful jack-of-all-trades in an isolated rural county: farmer, public school teacher, singing-school teacher, bandmaster, and auctioneer. ("The Snake-Chickens")*

MRS. EFFIE TURNEY BARNUM DEFOOR, *of Higden, Cleburne County, Arkansas, was born September 14, 1891, and related her story May 11, 1972. She is a second cousin of Roy E. Thomas, and granddaughter of a pioneer on the Little Red River, Abraham Turney. ("Early Beds")*

JIMMY DRIFTWOOD, *of Timbo, Stone County, Arkansas, is regarded by many as the outstanding folk musician of the Ozark Mountain region. A successful composer ("Battle of New Orleans," "Tennessee Stud," etc.), he has entertained in a dozen or more foreign countries, including the former Soviet Union, joined by his wife, Cleda, also an entertainer. He was born in 1906 and related his story about his grandfather November 6, 1970. ("Peddler Morris")*

LELAND DUVALL *grew up at Moreland, Pope County, Arkansas. He was born about 1908 and related two stories in September 1971. For several years he was a business and economics writer for the daily newspaper* The Arkansas Gazette. *("Leave a Hornets' Nest Alone!" and " 'That's the Way I Like It!' ")*

WILLIAM HENRY EARLY, *reared in the Caney community, Crawford County, Arkansas, was born in February 1876. He related his story February 26, 1971. He served in Cuba during the Spanish-American War and was living in a V.A. hospital, North Little Rock, when interviewed. ("Accidental Doctor")*

MRS. BELLE BUNCH FANCHER *grew up in the Liberty community, Carroll County, Arkansas. She was born November 7, 1885, and related her story April 21, 1971. Her husband was a livestock trader, and they were parents of six daughters and no sons. ("Box Suppers and Pie Suppers")*

ROBERT (ROB) FARRIS *was reared near Timbo, Stone County, Arkansas. He was born in 1891 and related his story February 22, 1972. ("On Laziness")*

JOE W. FUTRELL, *resident of Theodosia, Ozark County, Missouri, was born September 17, 1882, and related his story April 30, 1973. He played the fiddle, but not for dances. He built most of the caskets for people who died within ten miles of his home for years, never charging for that effort. ("Futrell and His Ferry")*

MRS. PEARL GARLAND *was postmaster at Salus, Johnson County, Arkansas, when she related her story, September 23, 1970. She was born about 1922. ("Two Sons Enter the Ministry")*

MRS. LULA HARRIS GUTHREY *was a resident of Cullman County, Alabama, born January 15, 1883. She was the wife of a farmer and related her stories March 29, 1977, in her ninety-fifth year. ("An Alcoholic Father," "Salt Shortage," and "A Southerner Who Did Not Believe in Confederate Cause")*

ERNEST CLINE HALTEMAN, *a farmer, lived at Quebeck, White County, Tennessee. He was born June 15, 1894, and related his story June 23, 1973. ("A Five-Year-Old Blackberry Picker")*

DAVID L. HAMPTON *was born at Protem, Taney County, Missouri, but had no permanent home growing up as an orphan. He followed his older brother to Indian Territory (now Oklahoma) but was scared of the good-natured Cherokee Indians. He was born June 18, 1873, and related this and several other stories May 4, 1973, in a nursing home a few weeks before his 100th birthday, in a two-hour interview. ("Two Snakes Trying to Swallow Each Other")*

MRS. EMMA SMITH HESS, *of Mountain View, Stone County, Arkansas, was born in 1881, and related her stories October 16, 1970. She and her husband, a farmer, were folk musicians. ("Souse, Also Called Headcheese" and "Cider Making")*

JESSE D. HINESLEY *lived near Fox, Stone County, Arkansas. He was born in 1886 and related his story November 19, 1970. He was an outstanding hunter and outdoorsman. ("The Dog That Climbed the Hollow Tree")*

MRS. MARGARET MOFFITT HOKE *lived in the Morganton community, Burke County, North Carolina. She was born June 3, 1893, and related her story December 29, 1975. The strong bond between her and her twin brother was remarkable. ("A Surprise Dinner Guest")*

HARVEY WALTER HORTON *grew up in the Nectar community, Blount County, Alabama. He was born December 28, 1880, and related his story March 30, 1977, in his ninety-sixth year. He was a farmer. ("Witching for Water")*

The Howard Sisters of Lamar, Johnson County, Arkansas, were born in the 1880s, and collaborated to tell their story. The sisters were MRS. ZELPHA HOWARD GARRETT, MRS. ROXIE HOWARD JOHNSON, *and* MRS. ELSIE HOWARD MANES. *("The 'Mule-colored' Mule")*

ULUS S. HUCKABY, *of Neck, Marshall County, Alabama, was born May 25, 1890, and related his story April 15, 1977. He was a drugstore owner. ("Neck, Alabama")*

MRS. EVELYN McINTOSH HYATT, *of Waynesville, Haywood County, North Carolina, was born June 26, 1885, and related her story October 4, 1975. She was a social historian and political activist. ("Voteless Indians Conscripted for Military Service")*

JUDGE (JUD) JOLLEY *was a farmer at Dennard, Van Buren County, Arkansas. He was born in 1891 and related his story October 14, 1970. ("The Hired Hand and the Old Hen")*

MRS. CORA BRAY BUCKNER KARR *grew up in Phelps County, Missouri. She was born April 20, 1889, and related her stories March 5, 1974. Her husband was a farmer. ("Brother Nep's Recitation" and "A Man and His Two Motherless Sons")*

ABE KING, *of the Harmony community, Johnson County, Arkansas, told the same story as Dillon O. Whitlow. He was born about 1912 and related his folktale September 23, 1970. ("Selling Chickens on Saturday")*

MRS. ROSA BEASLEY KIRK *lived at Ben Hur, Lee County, Virginia. She was born January 10, 1886, and related her stories June 27, 1975. She had a very vivid memory of her early life. ("Raising Flax for Linen" and "Making Candles")*

JOHN LEMARR *was a farmer who lived in the Lurton community, Newton County, Arkansas. An outstanding outdoorsman, he was born in December 1877, and related his story November 13, 1970. ("The Mule on the Bluff")*

MRS. NANCY ANNIE CLINE LUSK *lived at Pineville, Wyoming County, West Virginia. She was born May 27, 1879, and related her stories July 5, 1976. She was the daughter of a farmer and the wife of a sawmiller. In her ninety-seventh year, she was confined to a bed in a nursing home in Beckley, West Virginia, with a broken hip. She lived into her second century. ("A Girl Starts to School in 1886," "Woodchopper," "Woman Helped at Her Husband's Sawmill," "Love at First Sight," "Funeral Sermon Weeks after Burial," "Retribution: Knot on a Fiddler's Thumb," and "Great-grandfather at the Toll Bridge")*

FRED McCLELLAN *lived at Cass, Franklin County, Arkansas. He was born April 15, 1881, and related his story April 22, 1971, in his ninety-first year. He grew up and lived in what was to become the Ozark National Forest. ("Ember Days")*

FRED McCOY *lived at Wesley, Madison County, Arkansas. He was born in 1885 and related his story September 9, 1970. He was a farmer and a folk musician: he played the banjo at dances. ("Molasses Contest" and "The Birthday Party")*

JAMES (JIM) McGEE, *of Damascus, Van Buren County, Arkansas, was born in 1890 and related his story September 5, 1970. He served in combat in Europe in World War I. ("The Cat Story")*

MRS. ALICE HODGE McGUIRE *grew up on a farm by the Illinois bayou about eight miles west of Dover, Pope County, Arkansas. She was born in 1885 and related her story October 30, 1970. Her husband was a prosperous farmer who rented part of his large farm to tenants. ("Poke Sallet and Green Onions")*

MRS. VINA GILBERT METCALF *grew up in the Possum Holler community, Harlan County, Kentucky. She was born September 29, 1878, and related her story June 17, 1975, in her ninety-seventh year. ("Whiskey Is Good Medicine")*

EDWARD LIVINGSTON MILLER *lived at Conway, Laclede County, Missouri. A farmer, he was born April 1, 1885, and related his story February 27, 1974. ("Bitterness after the Civil War")*

THOMAS B. NORMAN *lived at Clarkrange, Fentress County, Tennessee. He was born November 7, 1884, and related his story June 30, 1974, a few months before his ninetieth birthday. His sense of history was quite good. ("Auction of Slaves")*

184

JOHN PAGE *grew up in Bullfrog Valley, northern Pope County, Arkansas. He was born in 1895 and was interviewed first in 1970 and three times after that. He was appointed postmaster at Hector, Pope County, by Franklin D. Roosevelt in 1933. At age ninety-eight, he was mentally and physically active in June 1993. ("Pretesting a Hired Hand")*

MRS. EUNICE FOUST SHEARER *was a lifelong resident of the Wilburn community, Cleburne County, Arkansas. Her husband was a farmer, then the postmaster. She was born in 1896 and related her story September 28, 1971. For several years Mrs. Shearer kept a personal diary, which was still unpublished at her demise. ("That Panther and the Baby")*

AUD SHOFNER *was a lifelong resident of Damascus, Faulkner County, Arkansas. His father was a machinist and held two U.S. patents for his inventions. Aud was a machinist, blacksmith, and innovator. He was born in 1900 and related his story November 6, 1970. ("The Automated Barn")*

MRS. MECY RELOFORD SINGLETON *lived at Sweet Home, Pulaski County, Missouri. She was born April 25, 1880, and related her story March 7, 1974, in her ninety-fourth year. Her parents were of Anglo-Saxon heritage; she was married to a son of two Swedish immigrants. ("Girls Went Fishing with Their Brother")*

MRS. LIZA ANN CARTER SMITH *was reared on Muddy Creek Mountain, Greenbrier County, West Virginia. She was born September 12, 1872, and related her stories June 2, 1976, in her 104th year. She was a daughter and wife of farmers. ("Sugarless Cake," "A Teenager's Flirtations, 1880s," and "A Corn Shucking, Followed by a Square Dance")*

WILLIAM COLUMBUS SMITH *lived at Parthenon, Newton County, Arkansas. He was born in 1880 and related his story October 14, 1970.*

185

He had been an active Baptist minister for fifty-seven years when he was interviewed; he was also an avid hunter for more than eighty years. ("A Wild Turkey Caught, Barely")

GEORGE STACY, *lifelong resident of Fairbanks, Cleburne County, Arkansas, was born October 2, 1896, and related his story in 1972.* ("The Unhandiest Things to Carry")

MRS. CATHERINE FITCH STOUT *lived at Neva, Johnson County, Tennessee. She was born April 12, 1872, and related her story April 29, 1975, in her 104th year. Her husband was a farmer and great hunter, and her father was a Union soldier during the Civil War.* ("Knitting Stockings and Socks")

J. EDWIN TICER *of Fox, Stone County, Arkansas, was born in September 1881 and related his story November 6, 1970. He was a farmer.* ("Dad's Yoke of Steers")

MRS. MARY ARMINTA WILKINSON TRASK *was born August 10, 1884, and* MRS. CORDELIA (CALLIE) RAYON WALKER *was born April 8, 1882. The two women lived in the Miami community, Ottawa County, Oklahoma, and had been friends for years. They were sharing a room in a nursing home at Miami when they were interviewed together in 1977; both contributed to the story.* ("Children and the Asafetida")

OSCAR UNDERWOOD *lived in the Harmony Grove community, Johnson County, Arkansas. He was born in 1883 and related his stories September 23, 1970. He was a farmer and never owned an auto.* ("Food in the Smokehouse" and "The Preacher Who Lost His Sermon")

MRS. CORDELIA (CALLIE) RAYON WALKER: see MRS. MARY ARMINTA WILKINSON TRASK.

JOE WARD, *resident of Optimus, Stone County, Arkansas, was born in 1894 and related his story May 12, 1971. He was a country schoolteacher and a farmer. During World War I, Mr. Ward, a white man, commanded a unit of black soldiers in the U.S. Army. ("'Ma, Whur's My Bed?'")*

MRS. ROY WARD *lived with her husband, a farmer, in the Wolf Bayou community, Cleburne County, Arkansas. She was born about 1896 and related her story May 11, 1971. ("Sidesaddles and Romance")*

WILLIS WARREN *lived at Ozone, Johnson County, Arkansas. He was born January 19, 1888, and related his story September 23, 1970. He was a farmer and also cared for many hives of honeybees. ("Making and Selling Chairs")*

MILES J. WEBB *lived at Lamar, Johnson County, Arkansas. He was born in 1890 and related his story May 14, 1971. His career work was as a rural mail carrier. He was blind when he was interviewed. ("Too Late to Learn")*

LEE WERT *spent his first fifty years at Cherry Hill, Perry County, Arkansas, and his next fifty-two in an all-black community of Menifee, Conway County, Arkansas. He was born in 1890, and interviewed in 1980 and 1990 and for a third time in 1993, at age 102 years. A longtime leader in his community, Mr. Wert is deeply religious and a moralist. ("Youth Worked at Barrel-Stave Mill")*

HORACE MAYNARD WHITE *lived at Braden Flats, Anderson County, Tennessee. He was born August 8, 1891, and related his story April 18, 1977. He was a coal miner from age thirteen to age sixty-eight. ("Convicts Worked in Coal Mines")*

FRANK WHITLEY *lived near Hartville, Wright County, Missouri, until 1920, when he moved to Los Angeles, where he had a successful* career as a real estate agent. He was a leader among the black real estate agents of California. He was born March 21, 1894, and related his story April 22, 1974. After his wife died, he returned to his roots in Missouri and waged an active but unsuccessful campaign in a Democratic primary as candidate to represent southwest Missouri in the U.S. Congress. ("Reading to My Parents, Former Slaves" and "A Family Moves in a Snowstorm")

DILLON O. WHITLOW *lived at Denmark, near the Independence County line, Arkansas. He was a successful farmer, hunter, and fisherman, born June 1883. He related his stories April 14, 1971. The first of his tales was also told by Abe King. ("Selling Chickens on Saturday" and "Neighborliness")*

MRS. FANNIE WHITTLE WILLIAMS *lived at Catoosa Springs, Catoosa County, Georgia. She was born October 19, 1882, and related her story August 19, 1975, in her ninety-fourth year. Her husband was a prosperous farmer. ("Progress: The First Screens on the Houses")*

JOE LEE WILLIAMS *lived at Centre, Cherokee County, Alabama. He was born December 18, 1880, and related his story August 15, 1975, in his ninety-fifth year. He was a farmer and a popular folk musician, playing any of four musical instruments for community dances. ("The Goat Fence")*

MRS. PEARL THOMAS WILLIAMS *grew up in the Enders community, Faulkner County, Arkansas, the youngest daughter of a country doctor and Methodist preacher. She was born in 1891 and related her stories October 14–16, 1971. She moved with her family to California about 1936, but she returned to Arkansas occasionally to see her siblings, nephews, and nieces. She was a sister of the father of Roy E. Thomas. ("Log Floors in Early Houses," "P-S-Y-G-K Spells Pie," "Small Houses," and "Something Good to Say about Everybody")*